3	4	5	6	7	8	9	10
0.83	0.75	0.68	0.62	0.56	0.51	0.47	0.42
0.76	0.66	0.57	0.50	0.43	0.38	0.33	0.28
0.69	0.58	0.48	0.40	0.33	0.28	0.23	0.19
0.64	0.51	0.41	0.33	0.26	0.21	0.17	0.13
0.59	0.46	0.35	0.27	0.21	0.16	0.12	0.09
0.55	0.41	0.30	0.22	0.17	0.12	0.09	0.07
0.51	0.36	0.26	0.19	0.13	0.09	0.07	0.05

$$= \begin{cases} 11\text{-}5\text{-}12 \\ + \sum_{1}^{N} 12 \end{cases}$$

NPV =
CUM'L.
DCF

INNOVATION

ИСТОЧНИКИ

INNOVATION

Managing the Development of Profitable New Products

Milton D. Rosenau, Jr.

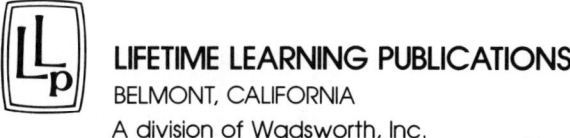

LIFETIME LEARNING PUBLICATIONS
BELMONT, CALIFORNIA
A division of Wadsworth, Inc.

London, Singapore, Sydney, Toronto, Mexico City

Jacket and text designer: Richard Kharibian
Editor: Sylvia Stein
Illustrator: John Foster
Composition: Computer Typesetting Services, Inc.

© 1982 by Wadsworth, Inc. All rights reserved. No part of this book may be reproduced, stored in a retrieval system, or transcribed, in any form or by any means, electronic, mechanical, photocopying, recording, or otherwise, without the prior written permission of the publisher, Lifetime Learning Publications, Belmont, California 94002, a division of Wadsworth, Inc.

Printed in the United States of America

1 2 3 4 5 6 7 8 9 10—86 85 84 83 82

Library of Congress Cataloging in Publication Data

Rosenau, Milton D., Jr.
   Innovation, managing the development of profitable new products.

   Includes bibliographies and index.
   1. New products—Management. I. Title.
HD69.N4R597 1982   658.5'75   82-13110
ISBN 0-534-97934-3

Contents

Preface xi

Part 1 Strategic Issues 1

1 **Strategic Planning** 3
   Reasons for New Product Development 3
   Reasons Against New Product Development 7
   Strategic Models 8
      General Electric Model 8
      Boston Consulting Group Model 9
      Arthur D. Little Model 13
      Lessons from the Models 13
   Highlights 14
   Further Reading 15

2 **A Unified Strategic Framework** 18
   The General Problem 18
   The Framework 19
   Criteria Screening 21
   Required Analyses 23
   Case Histories 24
      Pilkington Float Glass 24
      Perkin-Elmer Micralign 26
      Lessons from the Cases 29
   Highlights 29
   Further Reading 31

3 The Basis of Profitable New Products Development 32

Investment Outcomes 32
Case History 34
Research and Development Fallacies 36
   Integrating for Success 37
   Optimizing Research and Development Spending 38
Highlights 40
Further Reading 41

Part 2 The Market 43

4 Market Need 45

Inherent Needs 45
Postulated Needs 47
   Market Share Fallacy 47
   Needs Based on Technological Possibilities 47
Case Histories 48
   Structural Pressure-Sensitive Tape 48
   Pringle's Chips 49
Market Guidance for R & D Efforts 49
   Brainstorming 50
   Quick Estimates 51
   On-Line Information Retrieval 51
   Dyad Teams 52
   Market Research 53
Highlights 53
Further Reading 53

5 Market Research 56

Basic Issues 56
Case History 57
Crucial Market Research Issues 58
Case History 59
   Multiattribute Utility Analysis 60
   Focus Groups 62
   Timing 62
Performance of Market Research 63
Case History 64
Market Research Methods 66
Highlights 68
Further Reading 69

Part 3 The Product 71

6 Sources of Successful Ideas 73

Idea Origination 73
  Ideas Based on a Need 73
  Ideas that Capitalize upon Change 75
  Old Ideas 76
Improving Idea Generation 76
Licensing 77
Highlights 78
Further Reading 78

7 Evaluation of Ideas 81

Two Crucial Questions 81
  Can It Be Made? 82
  Can It Be Sold at a Profit? 83
Checklists 86
  Checklist Problems 87
  An Approach to Checklist Construction 90
Evaluation Issues 91
Case Histories 93
  Plumbing Innovations 93
  A Better Camera Lens 94
Highlights 95
Further Reading 96

Part 4 The Profit Plan 99

8 Financial Analysis 101

Program Financial Justification 101
Internal Rate of Return 103
Using the Profit MAP 105
  Required Data 106
  Determining Total Cash Flow 107
  Calculating the IRR 111
  Significance of IRR 112
  Sample Calculation 113
Comparison of Financial Measures 114
IRR Sensitivity to Estimate Assumptions 116
IRR as an R & D/Marketing Management Tool 116
Pricing Decisions 119
Effect of Premature Cancellation 119

Highlights   120
Further Reading   121

9   Uncertainty and Probability   124

IRR Probability Distributions   124
  Uncertainty   124
  Probabilistic IRR Distributions   125
Calculating IRR Ogives   127
  Gaussian Method   128
  Monte Carlo Method   129
Highlights   136
Further Reading   137

Part 5   Teamwork   139

10   The Role of Top Management   141

Annual Planning Context   141
Establishing New Product Development Phases   143
Establishing an Activity Flow   147
Reviews   148
Highlights   150
Further Reading   150

11   Organizational Issues   152

Ingredients of an Organization   152
Organizational Forms   154
  Functional Organization   155
  Matrix Organization   156
  Venture Team   157
External Ventures   160
Highlights   160
Further Reading   161

12   Improving Interface Harmony   164

The Disharmony Problem   164
Promoting Harmony   166
Highlights   168
Further Reading   168

Part 6 Summary 171

13 Concluding Remarks 173
New Product Success Criteria 173
Future Opportunities 174
Highlights 175

Appendix Contacts for Additional Assistance 179
Index 181

Preface

This book is about how to manage the development of profitable new products and improve the odds of their commercial success. It covers the essential issues in a simple, unified treatment that is complete and practical. This treatment is based on my twenty-five years of experience in high-technology engineering, marketing, and management of industrial and consumer products. The examples generally emphasize industrial products, but the principles apply equally to services and consumer products.

WHO THIS BOOK IS FOR

This book is for anyone involved in or interested in the development of profitable new products. More specifically, you will find this book valuable if you are:

- an engineering or R & D manager involved in developing new products. The book covers the five key factors of the process of developing profitable new products and explains the steps you must take to be an effective manager of such a process.
- a marketing manager working with technical managers. I provide vital insights into how to work effectively with engineering and R & D managers. You will find the basis

for a common understanding of what must be emphasized.
- a finance, manufacturing, or general manager in an organization that develops new products. You will see how your own actions must be integrated with the technical and marketing efforts. Then it will be clearer what actions all responsible managers must take to increase the odds that the new product development efforts will be successful.
- an investor in R & D limited partnerships. You will gain a better appreciation of the risks and how to reduce them.
- a venture capitalist or member of a board of directors. You will gain insights that will allow you to make more effective decisions.

THIS BOOK'S APPROACH

Managing the process of introducing profitable new products is complex. Although no treatment can or should make this process trivial, I make it as simple as possible. Thus, I segregate the five key factors I have found to be important: strategy, the market, the product, the profit plan, and teamwork. The overall new product development process is like a chain, so it cannot be more successful than the weakest of these five links. I carefully explain each of these five factors and indicate practical ways to cope with them. This segmentation has proven effective in both the successful development of real products and as a seminar outline for hundreds of working managers, so I am sure it will help you avoid the pitfalls in developing a profitable new product.

USEFUL AND UNIQUE FEATURES OF THIS BOOK

- Although there are many books on one or a few of the five key factors (for instance, strategy, market research, or teamwork), this book provides complete coverage of the entire subject.

- Each short chapter is devoted to a single topic and can be absorbed in an evening. Thus, the book is uniquely useful for the working adult.
- Numerous illustrations clarify key points.
- Case histories of both successes and failures are included to emphasize many issues.
- Checklists and flowcharts that you can adapt to your own situation are included.
- Each chapter includes annotated references to other recent publications if you would like to read more on any topic.
- The Appendix lists further contacts you may find helpful.

HOW THIS BOOK IS ORGANIZED

The book is divided into six parts. The first five are each devoted to one of the five key factors with which you must deal:

Part 1—Strategic Issues

The underpinning of any successful new product development effort is a corporate strategy. This tells you what you are trying to accomplish:

- What business are we in?
- What are we trying to accomplish?
- How do we propose to do this?
- Why do we want new products?

Unless you know what you are trying to do and how to get to that goal, you cannot know where to apply effort. This first part thus reviews common strategies (Chapter 1). Then I provide a simple framework you can use (Chapter 2). Finally, I identify some pitfalls to avoid (Chapter 3).

Part 2—The Market

After strategy, the next most crucial factor is the existence of a market need. A "problem idea" has to be created or recognized. You have to identify what the market need is or will be. Successful new products fill some need, even if it is only a created need. I first review how to identify such needs (Chapter 4). After that, I describe how to gather detailed information about product attributes that will allow you to develop a winning product (Chapter 5).

Part 3—The Product

The third factor in managing profitable new product development is to have a product or technological idea that sets you apart from the competition. This is a "solution idea." It answers the question of how you plan to capitalize upon the previously recognized "problem idea." It is not enough to recognize an unfilled market need; you must have a unique way to satisfy that need. Thus, I discuss how to come up with these ideas (Chapter 6) and how to evaluate them (Chapter 7).

Part 4—The Profit Plan

The fourth critical factor is a plan to make money. You can have a brilliant strategy, recognize an unfilled market need, devise a prize-winning product to satisfy that need, and still lose money. In this part I review how to decide if you can make enough money to justify the effort (Chapter 8). Then I show how to deal with the inherent uncertainty of predicting what will occur with your new product development effort (Chapter 9).

Part 5—Teamwork

Unless you are going to do the entire job alone, you will have to work with others. How are you going to get your profitable new product idea into the world? In general, meaningful new products emerge only from corporate teams of dozens, if not hundreds, of people working together. New product (and other) efforts are much more successful when harmony is promoted in such teams. In this part of the book, I first examine the crucial role that top management can play (Chapter 10). Then I look at some typical problems you can expect (Chapter 11). Finally, I describe ways you can improve teamwork (Chapter 12).

Part 6—Summary

The short last part of the book suggests where and how you should look for profitable new product opportunities yourself and identifies other continuing steps for you to take. It concludes with a highlight summary of key points.

ACKNOWLEDGMENTS

I gratefully acknowledge the experience I have gained from colleagues during my industrial employment, from my consulting clients, and from other management consultants. Many managers and executives at my new product development seminars have shared insights with me. I want to express my appreciation to all these people as well. The editor, Sylvia E. Stein, has done an outstanding job of clarifying my material. She has found better, shorter, and more lucid ways to express much of what I wrote. I am sure that the readers of this book will benefit greatly because of her work. Finally, Bruce Baird, William Giegold, John Heldt, John P. Klus, William E. Land, Alvin Murphy, and Robert J. Parden have provided insightful reviews of manuscript drafts, and I am deeply grateful for their time and knowledge. Clearly, any errors or omissions are my responsibility.

Milton D. Rosenau, Jr.
Santa Monica, California

INNOVATION

Part 1
STRATEGIC ISSUES

The underpinning of any successful new product development effort is a corporate strategy. It tells you what you are trying to accomplish:

- What business are we in?
- What are we trying to accomplish?
- How do we propose to do this?
- Why do we want new products?

Unless you know what you are trying to do and how to do it, you cannot know where to apply effort. Part 1 reviews common strategies in Chapter 1. Then I provide a simple framework that you can use in Chapter 2. In Chapter 3, I identify some common pitfalls.

1

Strategic Planning

KEY POINTS

You must know both where the new product development effort is expected to take the company and how the company will get there or you have no rationale for choosing new products to develop.

There are at least thirteen reasons that favor new product development.

There are at least six reasons why you should not engage in new product development.

Four general principles emerge from the three strategic models discussed in this chapter.

REASONS FOR NEW PRODUCT DEVELOPMENT

Before reading further, ask yourself why you should be engaging in new product development. Then ask if there are reasons you should not be doing it. In this book I presume that you or your company's top management has thoughtfully decided to undertake new product development. There are at least thirteen reasons for such efforts.

First there is a *product life cycle,* as indicated in Figure 1-1. It is inevitable that sales of all products will decline over some

Be sure you should be engaging in new product development before you undertake it.

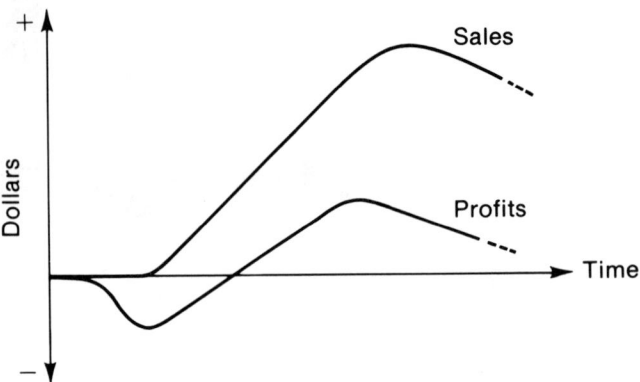

Figure 1-1. Product life cycle

period of time. The buggy whip is an obvious example. However, even a staple such as cane sugar stagnates eventually, for instance, because of artificial sweeteners. Another way to see this is illustrated in Figure 1-2.

A second reason is to respond to changed market conditions or to new legislation. For instance, if air bags are mandated for inclusion in automobiles, there will be a new market created

New		
Current	Will Decline in Future Years	
Markets / Products or Services	Current	New

Figure 1-2. All sales must come from current or new markets and products or services

for air bags. Some companies will be able to respond to that changed opportunity and become significant suppliers in the air bag market. In the case of legislation, a company must be careful that the legislation will not subsequently be changed or canceled. Such further legislation might very well take away the expected market before it develops fully.

A third reason to engage in new product development is to counteract the seasonality of a given product or to gain better capacity utilization within a company. As an example, ski manufacturers produce their skis in the spring or summer so they can get into the ski shop during the late summer or fall for sale to skiers. The ski factories are idle during fall and winter, giving the company poor capacity utilization. For this reason many ski manufacturers also produce products for summer and spring sports, such as water skis or tennis rackets.

Fourth, new product development can diversify a company. *Diversification* means entering new markets and simultaneously engaging in new technology, as illustrated in Figure 1-3. Diversification is extremely risky. Let us assume that today you are in the no-change cell with present marketing and technical requirements. Risk increases in approximate proportion to the number of lines that must be crossed. As a general rule, it is much smarter to make small changes in either the marketing or technical requirements. Then you digest these over a period of a few years; so this becomes the no-change marketing and technical requirements cell. Thus, over a period of many years you move in directions involving new marketing or technical requirements, but you do so in a series of small incremental steps rather than in one leap.

A fifth reason for new product development is to capitalize on a product that has come into a company and should be marketed. Sixth, and related to the fifth, is the sudden availability within a company of newer and more economical technology that can be exploited advantageously. Recently, McKinsey & Company, a management consulting firm, has popularized this sixth reason. They now refer to depictions of the technology life cycle as McKinsey S-Curves.

A seventh reason is to solidify a proprietary position in an attempt to gain market domination. In this case the company must stop short of a monopoly position in a major market. An eighth reason is some sense of social obligation to bring out a needed product. This altruistic reason (for instance, to serve ecological or educational needs) is often unprofitable.

Three other reasons companies engage in new product development are that it is a challenging or thrilling thing to do,

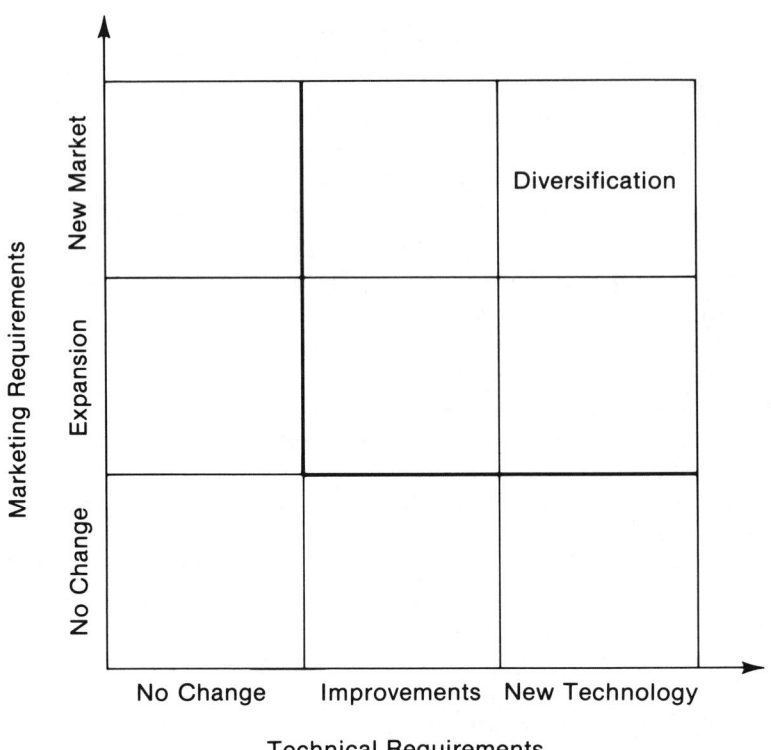

Figure 1-3. Diversification

that corporate image may demand such an effort, or for a sense of prestige. The Concorde supersonic transport was developed for some combination of these reasons. It is actually a subsidized convenience—heavily subsidized by Britain and France as a convenience for wealthy travelers. But it is a tremendous financial drain on the companies and countries that produced it: "The British Department of Trade said the costly Concorde supersonic jet will continue operating because it would cost too much to scrap it. It said the plane had already cost the taxpayers the equivalent of nearly $1.57 billion.... The committee described the elegant jet as a 'modern Frankenstein' monster whose costs were out of control... it would cost twice as much to scrap it as it would to keep it operating" (*The Wall Street Journal*, July 15, 1981, p. 24).

A twelfth reason for new product development is long-term survival of the company. Although this may be thought of as a variation of the first reason, this reason more commonly grows out of a long-term growth plan and the so-called planning gap,

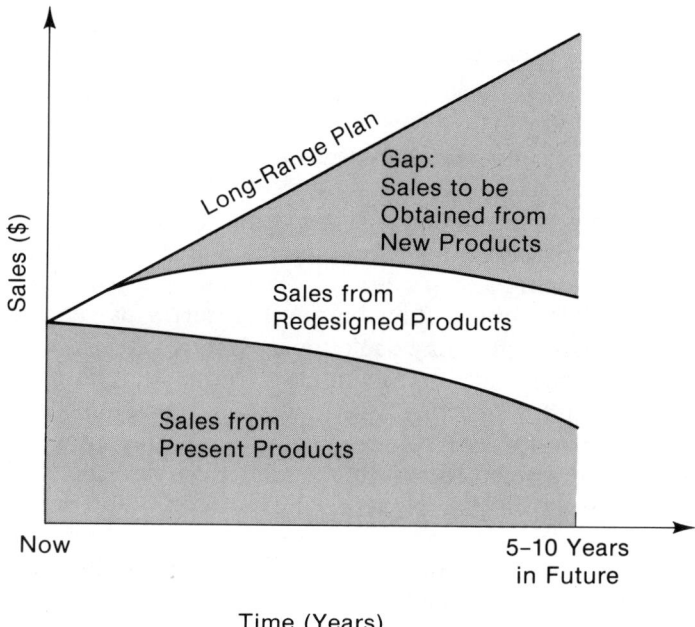

Figure 1-4. The planning gap

as shown in Figure 1-4. When companies engage in this kind of long-range planning, where it is considered essential to increase sales steadily in the future, a continuing flow of new products is called for. However, I believe the stress on increased sales is basically fallacious because the measure of long-range growth is taken as sales rather than profits or improvement on return on investment.

The last and most important reason for new product development is *profit* or *return on investment*. Improving one (or both) of these two factors is really the only reason for engaging in new product development. If this is not the basic reason your company is engaging in new product development, you should seriously ask yourself whether it is worth the effort.

The most important reason for new product development is to improve profits.

REASONS AGAINST NEW PRODUCT DEVELOPMENT

There are many reasons a company should avoid new product development. First, there may indeed be no market for the contemplated product. Second, there may be too much competition in the area the company is considering. Either of these reasons leads to a third general reason, which is that the cost is too high or there is no way to make money by engaging in the new product development effort.

Fourth, the risk may be too great or management may be too fearful of the effort to give it more than lukewarm support. For example, there may be unacceptably highly increased corporate liabilities or government regulations that would impede a company producing and successfully marketing a particular new product. Fifth, there may be another series of reasons such that the company may lack the required resources or technology to engage successfully in new product development efforts. For instance, the effort being considered may unacceptably dilute other efforts or compete with an existing company product. Thus, the new product might render obsolete an existing company product that presently has an acceptable profit level.

Sixth, there may be better alternatives to new product development. I enumerate some of these in the next chapter.

STRATEGIC MODELS

Many strategic models have been proposed. I describe three popular ones in this section. In the next chapter I propose a simplified and unified approach to strategic planning.

General Electric Model

The General Electric model encourages investment where your company has strength and the business is attractive.

The General Electric model for evaluating new product development investments is illustrated in Figure 1-5. Basically, this model indicates that investments and future growth are to be derived from areas in which the company has business strengths and where the businesses are attractive. Conversely, one should divest, or milk for profits, areas where the company is no longer strong or where the business is no longer attractive. In between these are situations that have to be decided on a case-by-case basis. This model is used as a guide to choosing areas in which to make new product development investments.

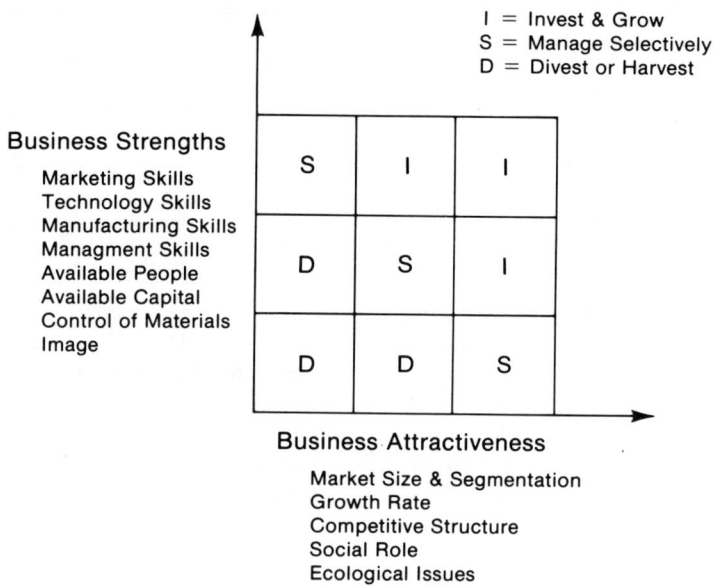

Figure 1-5. General Electric model

Boston Consulting Group Model

The basis of the Boston Consulting Group model is shown in Figure 1-6. The model begins with the observation that a company's cost of producing a product declines as the company accumulates experience. Although the declines vary in specific amount, an 80 percent *experience curve* is typical. That is, every time the quantity produced doubles, the company's production cost drops to 80 percent of what it was previously. Thus, as indicated in the right side of the figure, the largest producer has a dramatic cost advantage over another company that is producing less of the same product. For instance, if there are two companies producing a product and one has two-thirds of the market share and the second has one-third, the first company's costs are 80 percent those of the second (assuming an 80 percent experience curve). Alternatively, one can say that the second company, the company with the smaller market share, has costs that are 25 percent higher than the company dominating the market. The second parameter in the Boston Consulting Group model has to do with the growth rate of the market. Growth rate can also be measured by how much cash the company has to use. As we will see in Part 4, there is a greater cash use called for in a rapidly growing or expanding market.

The Boston Consulting Group model stresses the importance of having a dominant market share.

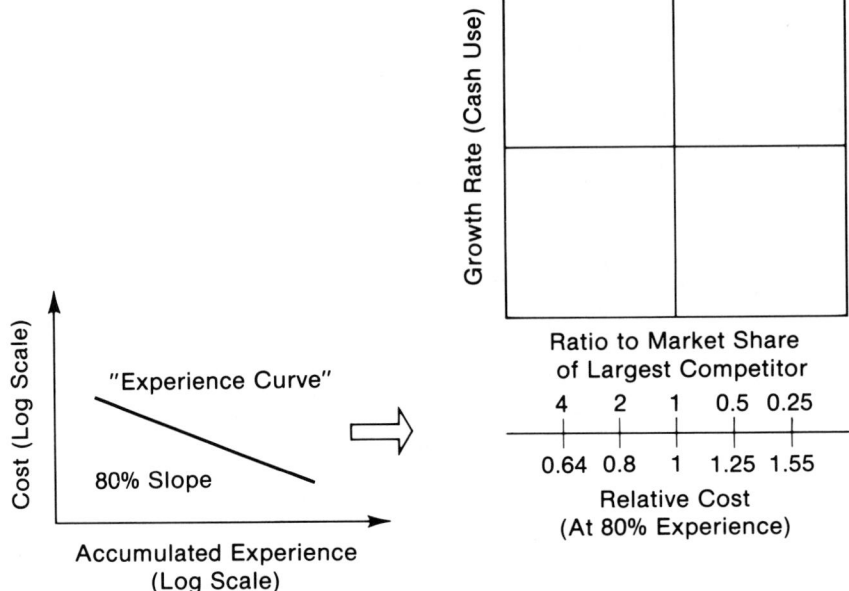

Figure 1-6. The basis of the Boston Consulting Group model

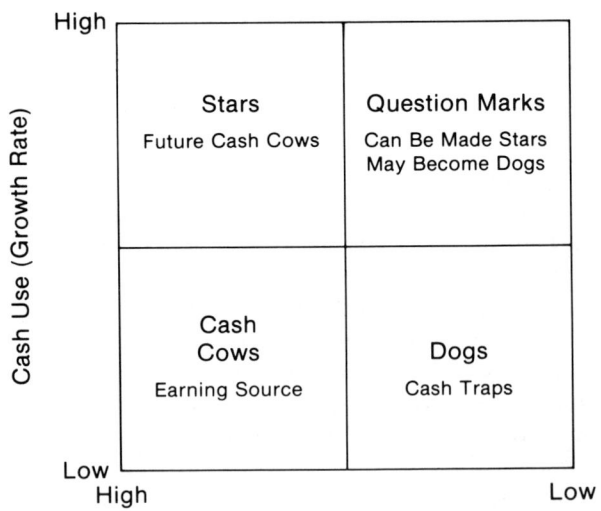

Figure 1-7. Boston Consulting Group model

Figure 1-7 is a picture of the resulting Boston Consulting Group model. Each of the four cells is characterized by certain kinds of products, each of which calls for a different managerial style. Low-growth markets, where a company has a high share, give you products called *cash cows*. They provide a lot of money to be used for other purposes. High share in a high-growth-rate market constitutes products called *stars* that will become cash cows when the market growth rate slows down.

The other two cells are where a company does not have a dominant market share. In a high-growth market these products are called *question marks*. They will become *dogs*, or *cash traps*, when market growth slows unless the company has some way to convert poor market share into good market share prior to slowing market growth. This model suggests strategic actions for using money for product management. They are indicated in Figure 1-8. Money from the cash cow should be applied either to speculative R & D or to question mark products, in which case the goal is to gain market share. From a product point of view, dogs should be divested and question marks should be moved into a situation where they become stars so that when the market growth slows, they will become cash cows.

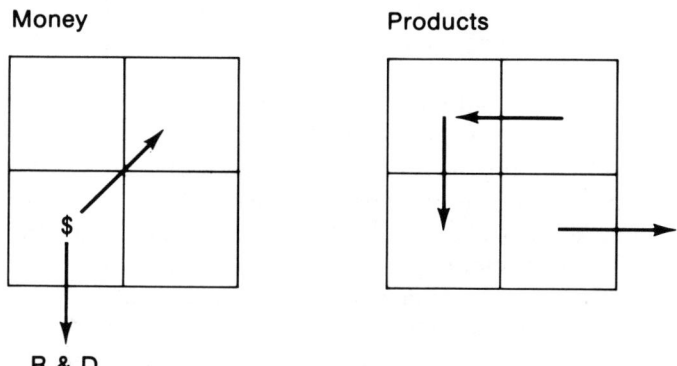

Figure 1-8. Strategic actions resulting from Boston Consulting Group model

The experience curve derives from four factors. First is the conventional learning curve. Second is the opportunity for specialization that leads to greater efficiencies. Third, as experience accumulates, there are efficiencies of investment that can

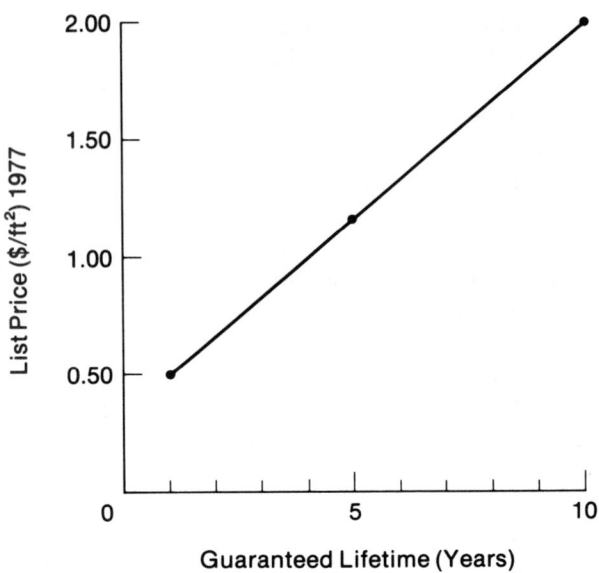

Figure 1-9. Market segments for retroreflective sheeting

be made. Fourth, the scale of the operation as it expands may be more efficient. These four reasons lead to the cost advantage that increased experience obtains from large market share.

Despite the popularity of the Boston Consulting Group model and its generalized validity, stressing the advantages of high market share, it has some problems. One is illustrated in Figure 1-9, which indicates that there are actually three products within the retroreflective sheeting market. Thus, when we talk about market share, the question is do we talk about the entire market or a segment of it. For instance, a segment might be the low-price, short-life market for retroreflective sheeting. This particular market is the so-called construction grade market, where the retroreflective sheeting is used for construction barricades. These barricades are frequently destroyed by cars hitting them or by careless workers who throw them off trucks. Long life is not an important product attribute for this market, but it is important for overhead routing signs.

Another potential problem with the Boston Consulting Group model is that one competitor in a market may have a different degree of vertical integration or capacity utilization. These factors may give the company costs different from those that the simple model would predict depending purely on volume. A third potential difficulty is that the money from the cash cows might be inadequate to move a question mark product to a star product. Similarly, the time for a star to become a cash cow may be too long for a company to endure. Finally, other factors may become significant. For instance, the manager appointed to manage a dog product may take that as a career signal to leave the company rather than moving to divest the dog product.

Arthur D. Little Model

Arthur D. Little, another management consulting firm, has developed a model in which twenty-four strategies are identified. Each of these has a natural period, depending on the stage of industry maturity: embryonic, growth, mature, and aging. As an example, one of their strategies is to produce new products for the same market. This strategy is appropriate in their model during the growth or maturing periods of market development. Alternatively, in the mature and aging phase of a product it might be appropriate to engage in backward or forward integration. During the embryonic and growth period, it might be appropriate to engage in the strategy of market penetration or the strategy of initial market development.

The Arthur D. Little model tries to match product options with product life cycle.

Lessons from the Models

Four general principles come out of these three models. First, the broad principles in each of these models are a helpful framework but not a specific prescription for actions to be taken by a company. Second, in general, there is an important advantage in the early phases to striving for market domination. Thereafter you try to take advantage of that domination during the mature phases. Finally, you must recognize that eventually it is important to get out of the business. Third, be sure that you are in attractive businesses where you have strengths and are not at a competitive disadvantage. Fourth, always know where in the development cycle you are and what your market position is. All this requires critical thinking and frequent exhaustively detailed reviews. The following list summarizes these principles:

1. Do not slavishly follow any "cookbook" rules, but do take advantage of established principles.

2. *Phase*   *Strategy*
   Early   Invest to gain dominant position
   Mature   Maintain average or dominant position
   Decline   Divest (harvest)

3. Stick to your knitting—in attractive businesses.

4. Know where you are—use critical thinking and exhaustively detailed reviews.

Understand your company's strategy.

Your company may already use one of these strategic models to guide new product development decisions. Perhaps they do not or perhaps you are not sure. The next two chapters cover related issues that should be part of your basic thinking. If your company's strategy is still unclear after reading the rest of Part 1, you must clarify the strategy to guide your work.

HIGHLIGHTS
Know why your company engages in new product development.

There may be very good reasons for a company not to engage in new product development.

Know on what model, if any, your company bases its strategy.

The General Electric model says to look for investments and future growth where the company has strength and the business is attractive.

The Boston Consulting Group model has two parameters: market share dominance and market growth rate.

The Arthur D. Little model matches product options and product life cycle.

The models provide a framework, not specific guides for action.

As a product goes through its phases, strategies must change.

Be sure you are not at a competitive disadvantage.

Always know where you are in the developmental cycle.

Always know your market position.

FURTHER READING

H. I. Ansoff and J. M. Stewart. "Strategies for a Technology-Based Business," Chap. 7, pp. 81–97 in R. R. Rothberg, ed., *Corporate Strategy and Product Innovation*, 2nd ed. New York: Free Press, 1981.
> This is a reprint of classic 1967 article on the relationship between strategy and technology.

R. A. Bengston. "Nine New Product Strategies: Each Requires Different Resources, Talent, Research Methods." *Marketing News*, March 19, 1982, pp. 7–8.
> This is a brief, somewhat superficial overview.

R. Biggadike. "The Risky Business of Diversification." *Harvard Business Review*, May–June 1979, pp. 103–111.
> Biggadike gives guidelines on how long it takes to bring new ventures to fruition and reasons to strive for high market share.

D. Bitando and A. Frohman. "Linking Technological and Business Planning." *Research Management*, November 1981, pp. 19–23.
> This article is a good review of ways to link R & D project selection to corporate strategic planning.

S. C. Brandt. *Strategic Planning in Emerging Companies*. Reading, Mass.: Addison-Wesley, 1981.
> This is a good, short overview of planning strategies.

B. Catry and M. Chevalier. "Market Share Strategy and the Product Life Cycle." *Journal of Marketing*, vol. 38 (October 1974), pp. 29–34.
> Here is a good discussion of the value of market share during the product life cycle, providing a link between the Boston Consulting Group and Arthur D. Little models.

P. Conley. "Experience Curves as a Planning Tool." Chap. 11, pp. 132–143 in R. R. Rothberg, ed., *Corporate Strategy and Product Innovation*, 2nd ed. New York: Free Press, 1981.
> This offers a good description of the Boston Consulting Group's experience curve.

C. M. Crawford. "Strategies for New Product Development." *Business Horizons*, December 1972, pp. 49–58.
> Crawford reviews the General Electric model and the necessity to have a new product strategy.

G. S. Day. "Diagnosing the Product Portfolio." *Journal of Marketing*, April 1977, pp. 29–38. Reprinted as chap. 12, pp. 144–

158, in R. R. Rothberg, ed., *Corporate Strategy and Product Innovation*, 2nd ed. New York: Free Press, 1981.
> This is a cogent discussion of the Boston Consulting Group model and its limitations.

D. Ford and C. Ryan. "Taking Technology to Market." *Harvard Business Review*, March–April 1981, pp. 117–126.
> This thought-provoking article tells how to milk more out of technology by recognizing the implications of the technology life cycle.

R. N. Foster. "Boosting the Payoff from R & D." *Research Management*, January 1982, pp. 22–27. "A Call for Vision in Managing Technology." *Business Week*, May 24, 1982, p. 24.
> Foster describes the McKinsey S-Curves.

R. H. Glazer and D. B. Montgomery. "New Products and Innovations—An Annotated Bibliography." Graduate School of Business, Stanford University, Technical Report 65, March 1980.
> This provides titles of 1960–1980 articles, many with annotations.

D. S. Hopkins. "New Emphasis in Product Planning and Strategy Development." *Industrial Marketing Management*, December 1977, p. 410–419.
> This is a very good review of the similarities in the three strategic models discussed in this chapter.

D. S. Hopkins. *New-Product Winners and Losers.* Conference Board report 773. New York: Conference Board, 1980.
> This is a study of the importance of new products and the rate of success in their introduction.

W. Kichel III. "New Management Strategies." *Fortune*, October 5, 1981, pp. 139–146; October 19, 1981, pp. 181–188; November 2, 1981, pp. 148–154; November 16, 1981, pp. 111–126.
> This four-part review of the shortcomings in existing strategic planning contains some indications of emerging thinking.

L. A. Murray. "The Product Growth Cycle for Electro-Optic Technologies." *Electro-Optical Systems Design*, October 1981, pp. 55–61.
> Some elements of the Arthur D. Little and Boston Consulting Group models are related to a specific industry.

R. T. Pascale. "Our Curious Addiction to Corporate Grand Strategy." *Fortune*, January 25, 1982, pp. 115–116.
> This is a plea to avoid having strategic models produce analytic detachment with a focus only on short-range profits.

S.J.O. Robinson, R. E. Hichens, and D. P. Wade. "The Directional Policy Matrix—Tool for Strategic Planning." Chap. 13, pp. 159–174, in R. R. Rothberg, ed. *Corporate Strategy and Product Innovation*, 2nd ed. New York: Free Press, 1981.

    They describe a modification of the General Electric model.

R. S. Rosenbloom and A. M. Kantrow. "The Nurturing of Corporate Research." *Harvard Business Review*, January–February 1982, pp. 115–123.

    The need to integrate long-range corporate R & D with basic strategy and some techniques to do so are discussed.

Y. Wind and V. Mahajan. "Designing Product and Business Portfolios." *Harvard Business Review*, January–February 1981, pp. 155–165.

    This is an excellent review of General Electric, Boston Consulting Group, and similar matrix strategies.

D. R. Ziemer and P. D. Maycock. "A Framework for Strategic Analysis." Chap. 7, pp. 87–105, in R. R. Rothberg, ed., *Corporate Strategy and Product Innovation*. New York: Free Press, 1976.

    This is a review of some of the issues in doing a strategic analysis.

2

A Unified Strategic Framework

KEY POINTS You must integrate your strategic plan with your new product development efforts.

There is a framework for successful new product development.

Further analysis may be required.

THE GENERAL PROBLEM

New product development has an uncertain success record. Estimates of commercial success vary from as little as one success in a thousand initiated projects to a high of two successes in three initiated projects. The imprecision of the project initiation process undoubtedly accounts for some of the variability. The risk of failure is less if you manage the process well; if you manage it poorly, failure is more likely. In either event, success is far from assured.

Success is never assured.

Some of the commercial failures encounter insurmountable technical hurdles or unfavorably altered market conditions. Other failures occur because there is no market or because the timing is wrong. Unfortunately, many failures occur because development is initiated without a plan to be profitable. That is, even if technical and market success is obtained, not enough money is earned to recoup the development expense. For instance, sometimes technical people become fascinated with some items of new technology and initiate a development effort. Sometimes marketing people get caught up in the competitive challenge without making a detailed plan with a high probability to make money. Occasionally a company does not have enough money to complete the development program. Some of this sloppy thinking is encouraged by or gets excused on the basis of "Let's play the hunches" or similar rationales. Although no one can fault the occasional success that occurs with this kind of approach, the odds favor a more orderly, self-critical one.

An orderly approach is helpful.

As I will discuss in greater detail in the next chapter, in many companies it is mistakenly believed that the research and development (R & D) effort is intended to spawn commercially successful new products. Unfortunately, a substantial portion of R & D effort is frequently devoted to other kinds of technical effort, for instance, routine quality control or customer technical service. Further, some of a company's R & D effort may be exploratory and not immediately aimed at making a profit. The dollars devoted to such a budget may be very large in giant companies. In one case over $20 million was allocated in 1978 to a speculative R & D program in an extremely large multinational company. But this kind of speculative or exploratory R & D activity does not have profitable new product development as the immediate, primary objective. Rather, the primary goal is the discovery of fundamental new knowledge that may be commercially useful at some future time. Thus, these budgets must be justified on other bases, and such programs must be evaluated in other ways.

THE FRAMEWORK

Figure 2-1 illustrates the framework in which a successful new product development strategy can be set. This framework cannot guarantee success, but it can minimize unnecessary failure. The entire effort starts with a corporate profit plan and strategy. (Although some companies may opt to reduce their profits or hold them steady over periods of time, this book is concerned with those companies that wish to increase profits.) A perfectly adequate short-range strategy is to manage the existing business better. In fact, it is a rare company that cannot

A corporate profit plan and strategy are the first step.

20 Strategic Issues

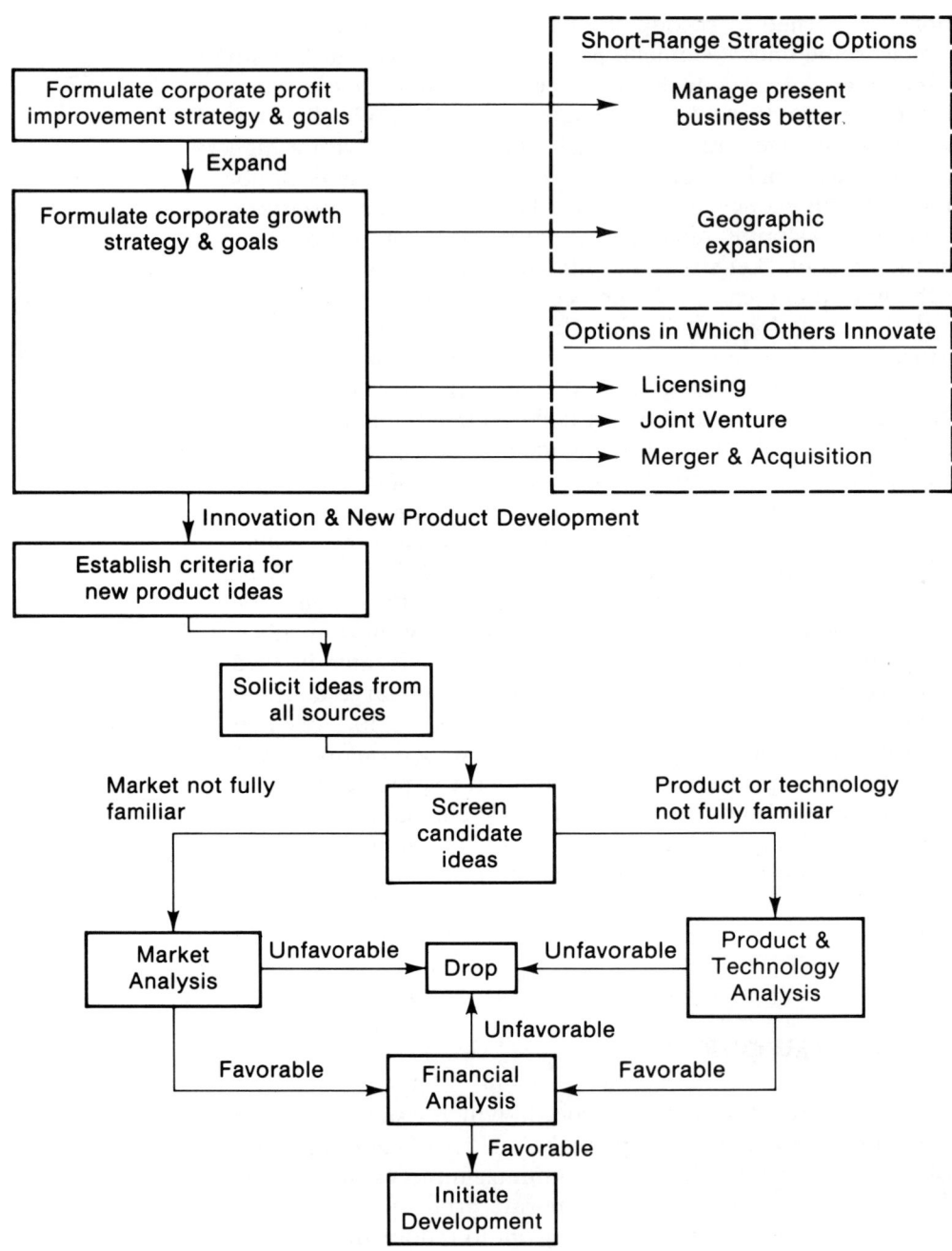

Figure 2-1. Framework for successful new product development

improve its current operations. Unfortunately, this will eventually run into the law of diminishing returns, making it necessary to adopt some kind of expansion strategy.

When the expansion strategy for the company is considered, there are several options. Geographic expansion is a short-run strategy that will eventually result in market saturation. Licensing, joint ventures, or merger and acquisition options are all viable expansion strategies, but they are short range in the sense that they ultimately depend upon some other organization to be successful in new product development. Thus, a company must ultimately face the necessity to become proficient at new product development if it wishes to increase profits over some lengthy period.

With contemporary inflation levels and the concomitant high cost of money, new product development may be temporarily more expensive than some of the alternatives. For instance, it is now common to seek a merger, especially if the merged company has a depressed stock price. These conditions are abnormal. Even in the current situation many companies still find it most attractive to expand by new product development. Such companies are willing to perform the critical analyses that must be an integral part of development efforts and that allow them to reduce the inherent risks and thus improve the prospect of success.

CRITERIA SCREENING

Although the first three steps in criteria screening are straightforward, companies frequently omit them. It is not uncommon that some bright-eyed, frequently articulate, and certainly persuasive member of the R & D or marketing department advocates a pet idea. Very often a great deal of momentum is built up behind this idea without any framework in which to consider it. Ideas in which the company has neither market nor technological experience often appear particularly alluring because nobody in the company has enough information to identify the serious flaws inherent in them.

Thus, corporate management should establish criteria for new ideas. As a minimum, these criteria should establish market, product or technology, and financial standards against which ideas will be judged. Other policy criteria may also be incorporated. If the management of an instrument corporation

First, establish company criteria.

does not wish to be in the cement business, for instance, this should be clear from the adopted criteria. Criteria must not be so stringent that no idea short of a perfect one can satisfy the standards. Part 1 of this book is devoted to helping you establish criteria.

Second, solicit ideas from everyone.

Second, as many alternative options as can easily be gathered should be solicited. These should be sought both internally and externally. This is an area in which outside consultants can frequently be invaluable, particularly if the company wishes to make an external survey anonymously. Part 2 of this book helps you look at market needs critically.

Third, screen the ideas critically.

Third, these options should be systematically screened against the criteria to find the most promising ones, as shown in Figure 2-2. It is not uncommon that an idea will require a quick study to clarify some uncertainties. By all means make a quick study, but do not allow it to escalate into a full-blown development effort until such an effort is formally approved. Part 3 of this book suggests ways to screen ideas, and Part 4 shows you how to decide if you can make money.

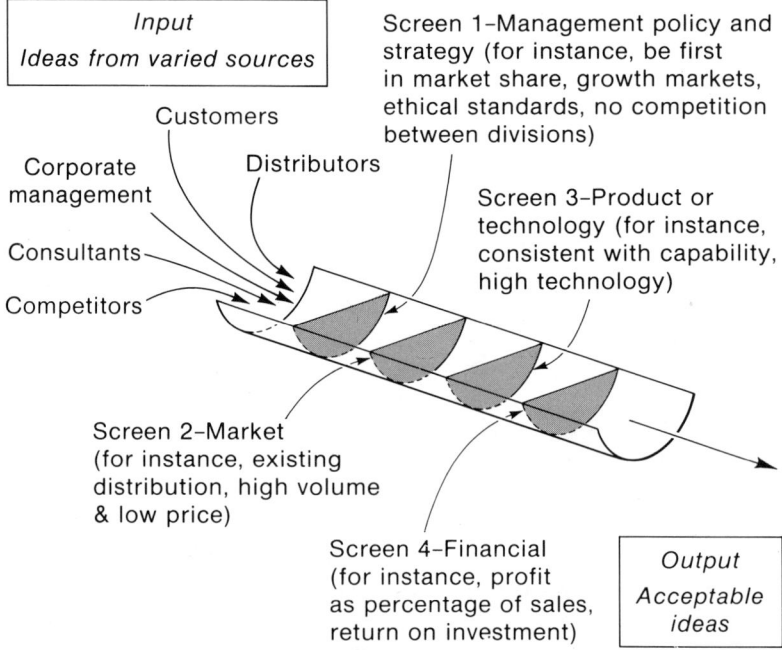

Figure 2-2. Application of screening criteria

REQUIRED ANALYSES

If either the product and technology or the market is not fully familiar, they should be subjected to a reasonable degree of further analysis. If that analysis is unfavorable, the idea should be dropped. At most the advocate may be allowed a very short grace period in which to demonstrate that the unfavorable judgments are mistaken. But because dropping an unpromising idea in which some investment has already been made is painful, many poor ideas are allowed to continue to absorb money and resources.

If, however, the idea is judged to be favorable on both scores, then a preliminary financial analysis should be conducted. If that is favorable, it is then appropriate to initiate a development effort. This is the kind of development effort upon which money and resources should be concentrated.

Concentrate limited resources on a few potential winners.

Once the development effort has been initiated, it is necessary continually to reexamine the market, the technology or product, and the financial plans. It is normally wise to test the idea (or pilot product) frequently with potential users because this introduces market reality. For instance, with regard to the marketing aspect, either a need must exist in the marketplace or there has to be a plan to create such a need. In the latter case, there should be a budget for the effort that will lead to creation of a need. The cost of this marketing effort as well as other development expenses must be consistent with the expected rewards.

Ideas must pass market, technical, and financial tests.

Figure 2-3 indicates the necessity for you to have both a high degree of technical or product and market information about an idea. Technical people often ignore the market entirely and continue to invest their efforts in improving the technology (see Figure 2-4). Time spent in this manner moves the program further from the region of balanced knowledge in which commercial success is possible. This does not mean, of course, that some efforts will not be successful purely by accident. Accidental success is fine when it happens, but counting on it is a poor way to operate. Balanced knowledge is crucial for a corporation, particularly a publicly owned one in which the senior management has a fiduciary trust to the stockholders.

Figures 2-5 and 2-6 show the kind of financial analyses that are appropriate at different stages of the effort. It is entirely satisfactory to use something as simple as the back of an envelope at the initial stages. Before any major investment is made, it is vital to do a *discounted cash flow*, which is covered in Part

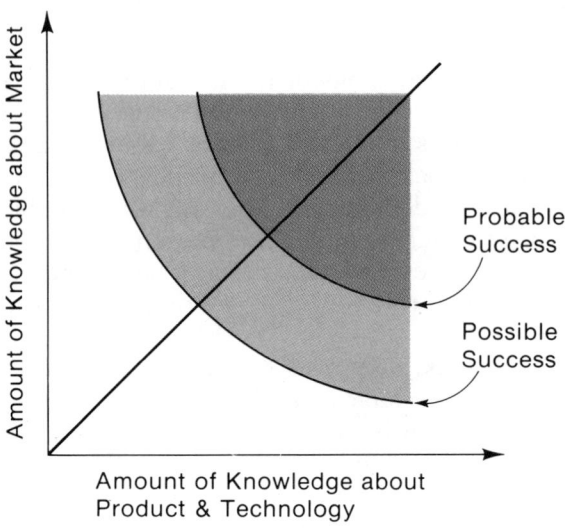

Figure 2-3. Need for balanced knowledge

4. This allows you to calculate *internal rate of return* (IRR) or *net present value* (NPV) so that the time value of money is taken into account. After the product has reached the market, concentration on profit margin becomes appropriate. *Return on investment* (ROI) can be measured after the development investment has been recovered.

CASE HISTORIES

Pilkington Float Glass

One of the great commercial development success stories of the last three decades is the development of float glass by Pilkington. When the project started in 1952, there were two kinds of window glass available. The first was sheet glass, which was inexpensive and was polished by running it under a hot flame. This process left various inclusions or irregularities in the glass and thus provided a distorted view. Distortion-free glass was quite expensive because it required running the glass under twin grinding and polishing heads. This process produced glass that was without inclusions in the surface and resulted in smooth surfaces. Pil-

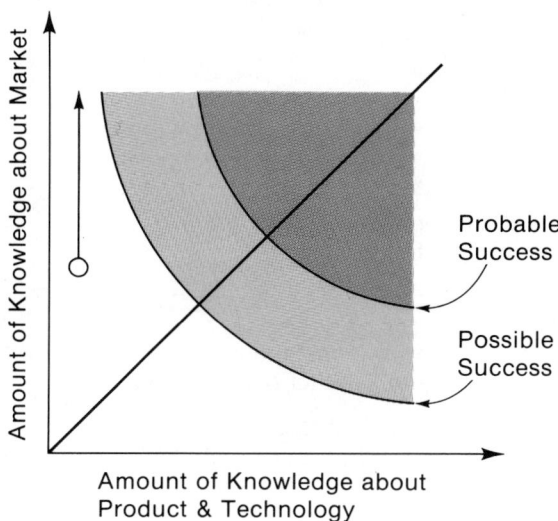

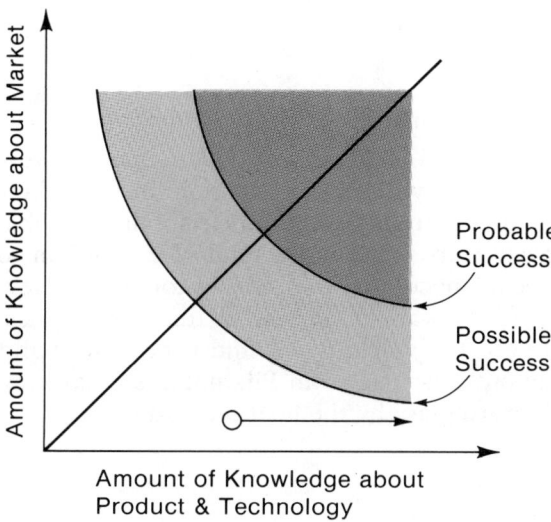

Figure 2-4. Failure modes

kington's goal was the quality of twin ground glass with the economy of sheet.

The broad notion for accomplishing this was to float mol-

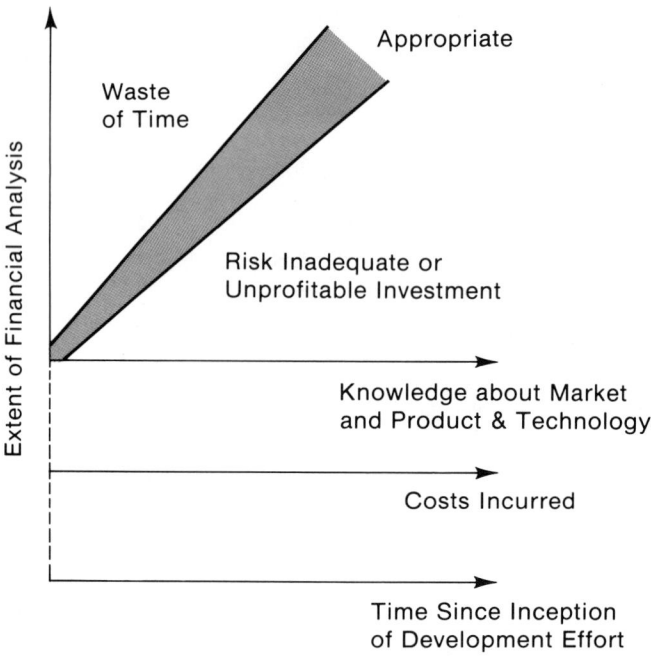

Figure 2-5. Financial analysis effort

ten glass on molten tin. Then the glass would settle due to the action of gravity and have perfectly plane parallel surfaces. It took over seven years and £4 million (in those days a very large amount of money) to produce the first salable glass. It took even more time and a total of £7 million to achieve commercial success on the basis of low price. Nevertheless, the process was so successful that every glass-making company in the world has found it necessary and desirable to take out a license from Pilkington so that they, too, can manufacture glass by the float method.

Perkin-Elmer Micralign

Another tremendous commercial success is the Perkin-Elmer Micralign instrument (Micralign is a trademark of The Perkin-Elmer Corporation). As indicated in Figure 2-7, the means by which semiconductor wafers were made in the mid 1960s was by contact (or near contact) printing. In this process the glass artwork master was pressed against

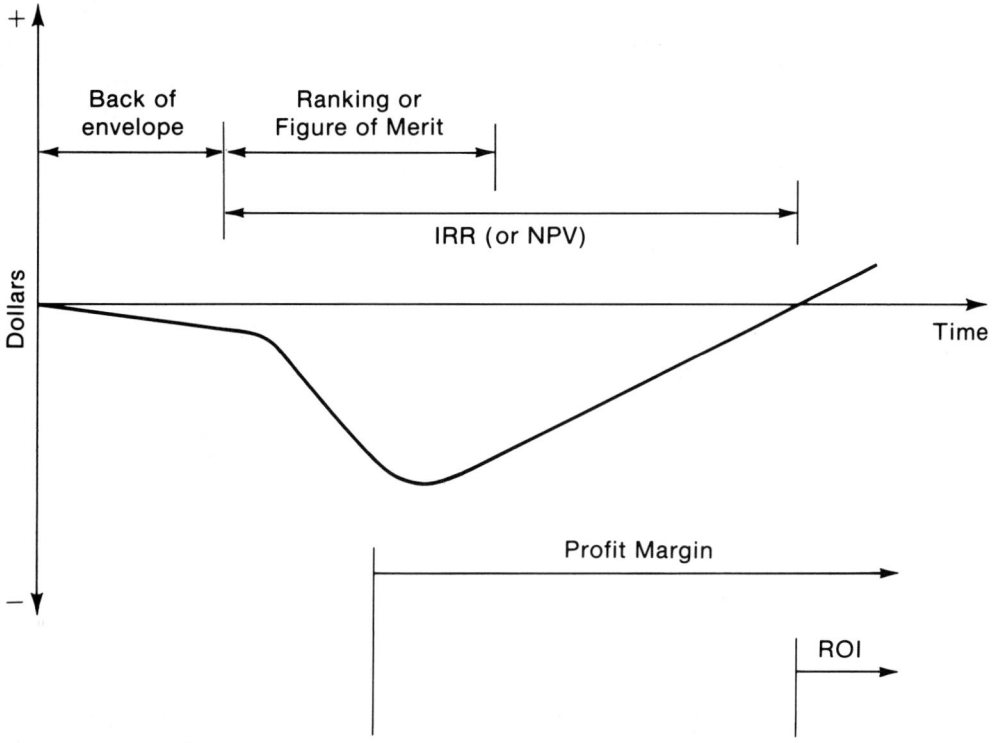

Figure 2-6. Appropriate financial analyses

(or put in close proximity to) the silicon wafer on which the microlithographic patterns were to be etched. (Near contact printing is capable of making only coarse pattern circuits, which severely limits its utility as a production option.) Multiple exposure and processing steps are called for to develop even modestly complex circuits. It was not uncommon in more complex circuits to go to six or twelve contact printing steps with successive developments and other processing steps involved, which led to serious problems in the semiconductor production industry. The glass artwork masters, which were very expensive, were abraded by being placed in contact with the wafers. Thus, these expensive masters had a very short life. Second, the wafers tended to deform during multiple exposure steps. Consequently, they bent in a way similar to a potato chip, but to a much smaller extent, and when they were pressed in contact with the original artwork master, they broke.

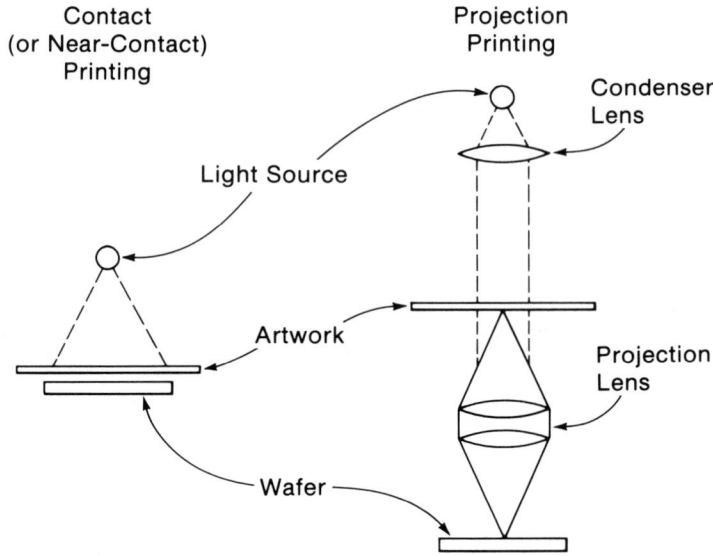

Figure 2-7. Perkin-Elmer Micralign

People in the semiconductor industry understood these problems. They persuaded the U.S. Air Force that it would be to its advantage to sponsor development efforts. The expectation was that projection printing would lower the Air Force's cost of required semiconductor devices. In the face of severe competition, Perkin-Elmer obtained two Air Force contracts to begin to attack this problem. These efforts were under way from 1967 through the end of 1970. Basically what happened was that Perkin-Elmer learned how *not* to produce a projection printing instrument under Air Force sponsorship. Thus, their risk in undertaking a commercial development effort, commencing in 1971, was greatly reduced. Perhaps the most important lesson learned during the Air Force sponsorship was that a refractive projection lens (one may think of this as a unity magnification photographic enlarger) would not be sufficiently good for this purpose. Rather, it was clear that the projection lens had to be entirely reflective because it could not be a refractive lens. It was also learned that the condenser lens used to illuminate the artwork had to be of very, very high quality. Thus, when the commercial development effort was started, using Perkin-Elmer's own development monies, it was clear what characteristics were important to stress in the instrument. Further, Perkin-Elmer had been educated in and developed knowledge of the nature of the semiconductor market.

As in the Pilkington case, commercial success required many years. Micralign sales reached about thirty units (worth $4–5 million) per month in 1977, a decade after the first Air Force contract. It was 1980 before sales volume reached $100 million per year.

Lessons from the Cases

Earlier in this chapter I stressed the importance of having a balanced amount of knowledge about the market as well as the product and technology (Figure 2-3). Figure 2-8 qualitatively shows how Pilkington and Perkin-Elmer started out in very different ways with different kinds of knowledge, but both companies' efforts led to commercial success. When Perkin-Elmer started their efforts, they knew a great deal about the technology of high-performance optical instruments, but they were not in the semiconductor market. Initially, they gained some knowledge about the market from the Air Force contract and also learned that they had to improve their technology. Later they hired market researchers to teach them more about the semiconductor market. They thus proceeded in a series of small steps, primarily emphasizing gaining knowledge about the market while making small improvements in the product to serve the market best.

Pilkington, as a major supplier of sheet glass, knew essentially everything they had to about the marketplace. Their entire effort was therefore concentrated on improving their product and manufacturing technology rather than on conducting market surveys. Both companies achieved balanced amounts of knowledge and tremendous market success. This should be your goal.

HIGHLIGHTS

Companies must engage in new product development for long-range profit growth.

Success requires a balanced knowledge about the product and technology as well as the market, and this knowledge must become increasingly thorough as the development effort progresses.

30 Strategic Issues

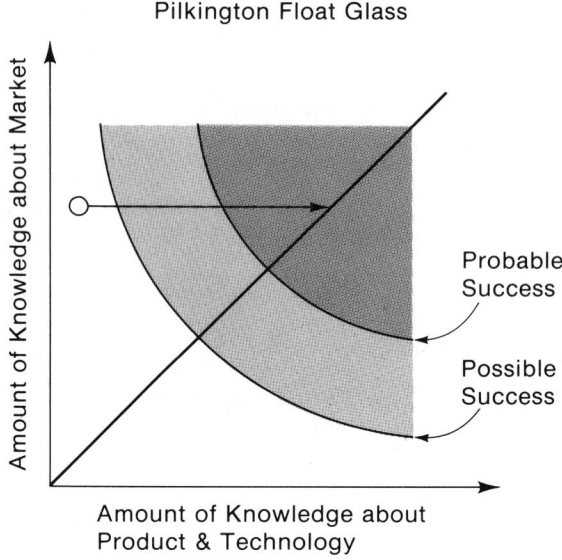

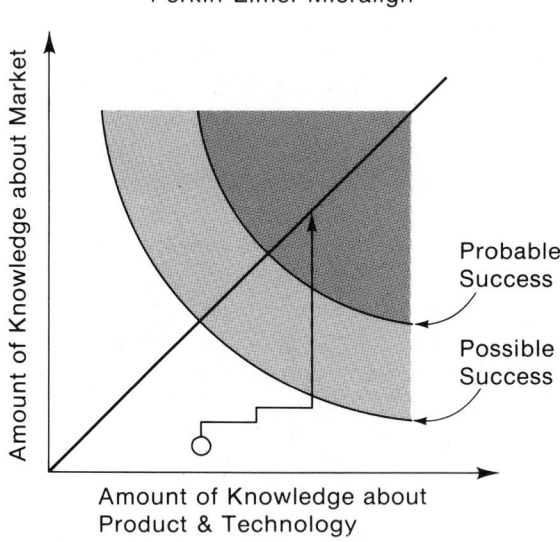

Figure 2-8. Two success patterns

Financial analyses, which become increasingly detailed and must promise that considerably more money will be earned than is spent, must also be conducted.

A strategic model is helpful in deciding what actions to take. Its essential elements are criteria for new product development, solicitation of ideas from diverse sources, and systematic screening of ideas against at least market, technical, and financial standards.

FURTHER READING

F. R. Bacon, Jr., and T. W. Butler, Jr. *Planned Innovation*. Ann Arbor: Industrial Development Division, Institute of Science and Technology, University of Michigan, 1981.
> *They offer another approach to establishing a strategic framework that is generally similar to that described in this chapter.*

G. Kinkhead. "The Raging Bull of Glassmaking." *Fortune*, April 5, 1982, pp. 58–64.
> *This article about Guardian Industries has much information about the Pilkington float glass process.*

E. P. McGuire. *Evaluating New-Product Proposals*. Conference Board report 604. New York: Conference Board, 1973.
> *This is an excellent review of methods companies use to judge the relative merits of candidate new product efforts.*

E. B. Lovell. "Licensing: Reasons, Royalties, Dangers." Chap. 8, pp. 106–120, in R. R. Rothberg, ed., *Corporate Strategy and Product Innovation*. New York: Free Press, 1976.
> *Lovell reviews how licensing fits into strategic planning.*

L.A.B. Pilkington. "The Float Glass Process." *Proceedings of the Royal Society of London*, vol. 314 (December 16, 1969), pp. 1–25.
> *This is the classic description of how the Pilkington float glass process was developed.*

J. B. Quinn. *Strategies for Change*. Homewood, Ill.: Irwin, 1980.
> *This good book on strategy has more information on Pilkington.*

The Basis of Profitable New Product Development

KEY POINTS Avoid investing in efforts that will fail or failing to invest in efforts that will succeed.

Do not entrust new product development to the R & D or engineering groups.

INVESTMENT OUTCOMES

Table 3-1 illustrates the outcomes you can expect as a result of the decision to invest or not invest effort in new product development. A principal goal of this book is to help you make money, that is, to avoid investing in efforts that are foredoomed to failure. Thus, the book is designed to increase the likelihood that you will make a correct decision and not invest in product development efforts that can result only in failure. However, whenever a decision is made to invest in a particular product development, there is always some risk that the effort will fail (for instance, due to unforeseen events). Likewise, a decision not to invest means a risk of lost opportunities. If you apply the principles enumerated in this book, you are more likely to in-

TABLE 3-1. Product Development Investment Outcomes

		After the fact—If product development is completed it would be	
		A Failure	A Success
Before the fact—Corporate decision is to	Not Invest	Correct Decision	Lost Opportunity
	Invest	Lost Money	Correct Decision

vest limited resources in successful product development efforts that will make money.

Always remember, however, that only one thing is sure. Once you start a new product development effort, you will be confronted with the certainty of expense—in terms of both human effort and money.

Expense is the only certainty in new product development.

Various studies of successful new product development efforts have been conducted. The results range from one success in a thousand to two in three. The statistic quoted depends on what you count as an initiated effort. If the enunciation of an idea that is dropped later in the afternoon is counted as an unsuccessful effort, it is more likely that one in a thousand ideas is successful. Conversely, if a new product development effort starts with a concept that is well formulated in some market research and for which a prototype exists, then perhaps two in three new product development efforts are successful. Every corporation has limited resources; so your goal must be to focus or concentrate limited resources on a few new product development efforts, preferably those that have the highest likelihood of being successful.

Concentrate limited resources on a few prospective winners.

You must also understand that success is never certain. First the product development effort itself must be completed technically. Then the product must be commercialized. Finally the product must be successful in the marketplace. Each of these three steps has less than 100 percent certainty of success. Therefore, the probability of market success, assuming that the product development effort was initiated, must also be less than 100 percent certain. Think about it like a chain with a series of links. Any weak link in the development process will lead to a new product development failure.

New product development is inherently uncertain.

In a sense this book is about risk minimization. Nothing I can write will show you how to get ideas that have guaranteed success. But I can and do indicate the methodology and steps that will help you improve your company's performance. At its simplest, five factors are involved:

1. A basic business strategy
2. A market need or concept
3. A product or technical idea
4. A plan to make money
5. Teamwork on the part of various participants

You require a market need or concept and also a product idea.

Ideas are involved in two different ways in this process. Initially, there has to be a *problem idea* to which the candidate idea for the market need or concept is addressed. Later, when there is some plausible market target identified, there has to be a *solution idea*, that is, a product that is in some way unique, novel, or otherwise differentiated from other possible solutions that address this first conceptual need. In general, the best of the problem ideas come from acute observation of the outside world. The solution ideas come from the creative processes, such as brainstorming or technical invention. One of the fallacies that bedevils new product development is that R & D or other technical personnel, such as development engineers, should come up with creative ideas for new product development. Unfortunately, such technical ideas exist in a market vacuum and are most likely to lead to unsuccessful efforts. Finally, assuming that problem and solution ideas exist, you must expect that much more money will be made by undertaking the new product development program than will be spent during the program.

CASE HISTORY

In 1972, an engineer working for a high-technology company was taking a spring vacation in Washington, D.C., with his family and went on a tour at the Bureau of Engraving and Printing. He noticed that a very large number of workers were inspecting the front and back of currency notes for the purpose of finding defects. He wondered if the process might be automated. At this point there was an observation of the outside world and the germ of a concept. His own thinking at that point was that a photographic image could be made of a perfect dollar bill and a negative of that photograph could then be superimposed on the currency notes as they were being inspected. This technique, with which his company was then familiar, is called optical correlation. It is an extremely simple and powerful technique for locating mismatches between supposedly identical flat objects.

Subsequent investigation revealed the precise definition of a defect on the currency note: the presence of ink where it should not be or the absence of ink where it should be. The size of a defect was approximately 0.1 millimeter. Unfortunately, the Bureau of Engraving and Printing had already hired a contractor to explore this optical correlation possibility. They found that the correlation approach would be hopeless because the dimensional stability of currency notes is only about 1 millimeter due to paper shrinkage and expansion caused by temperature and humidity changes.

In talking with the Bureau of Engraving and Printing, the company's commercial marketing manager, who was now directing the venture, learned approximately how many people were engaged in inspection. Multiplying the number of inspectors by their estimated salary and fringe benefits provided an estimate of the value of a solution. This inspection cost was a large fraction of the cost of producing currency notes. The marketing manager estimated that solving this problem was worth a few million dollars to the Bureau of Engraving and Printing. Presumably other central banks (such as England, Germany, and Japan) would have a comparable interest in the solution of this problem. Thus, the marketing manager could make a preliminary estimate of the worldwide market with central banks. Further talk revealed that smaller countries get their currency notes printed by commercial printers (two large ones and one smaller one of some significance). Visits to two of these commercial printers confirmed that they, too, had the same inspection cost problem. These visits also revealed that there was a still larger market for other security documents, especially the inspection of traveler's checks. Now the marketing manager could estimate the amount of worldwide labor devoted to inspecting security documents. The size of the potential market for equipment to replace this labor was significant.

Further investigation revealed still another market: playing cards. The front and back of every playing card has to be inspected for defects. A defect on the back produces a marked card; a defect on the front is a quality defect. At the largest producer of playing cards, four hundred out of thirteen hundred employees did nothing but inspect the front and back of playing cards. Estimating that company's market share in worldwide production enabled the marketing manager to estimate how much labor was devoted to this activity. He now knew that the market value of labor devoted to inspecting printed documents represented several tens of millions of dollars. This indeed was an attractive market need to go after. His company had a firm market concept in mind. There was now a real problem to try to solve.

The company also knew enough to know that the simple approach of optical correlation was not going to solve the problem. At this point a larger group of technical people became involved and were asked to try to invent some solutions to the problem. They did so. The most promising solution was to divide the document up into patches small enough so that each one's dimensional instability was small compared to the size of the defect. Then it was possible to practice optical correlation as these small patches were sequentially moved around. This motion then covered the entire surface of the particular document.

This case illustrates the successful, iterative actions that get a company through two of the steps of a successful new product development effort. Subsequent efforts were required to come up with a plan to make money and to develop a harmonious teamwork relationship between the various departments involved in the program. In common with the examples in the previous chapter, over a decade was required to get into the market. But the result was impressive: "Compared to current hand inspection techniques, the system operates with greater precision, at a more consistent level of quality, and at lower cost" (*Electro-Optical Systems Design*, July 1981, p. 12).

RESEARCH AND DEVELOPMENT FALLACIES

Attitudes such as these are typical of many misguided company new product efforts:

Research and Development Fallacies

- "Let R & D do it."
- "R & D is supposed to come up with new products."
- "Why don't we get a return from all the money we spend on R & D?"

Sometimes the misguided attitude is directed toward the development engineers. (For simplicity, I will use R & D as an example for the rest of this chapter.) There are two fallacies underlying these attitudes. First, R & D, in a vacuum, should come up with new products. Second, R & D effort is correlated in some way with innovation and subsequent profits.

Integrating for Success

The first fallacy is rooted in one of the central points in this book, namely, that teamwork, not just R & D, is required. Success requires an integration of the following:

1. A need or a problem idea (in which marketing should take the lead)
2. An innovative idea that responds uniquely to the need or a solution idea (in which R & D, engineering, or product development should take the lead)
3. A profit plan, namely, a realistic notion of how to make more money than the development will cost

I know of companies where some senior manager turns to R & D and says, "You are the future of our company; come up with innovative new product ideas." In general, the best skills of R & D people are not selecting the problem upon which to work, but rather in coming up with clever solutions to problems posed to them. Thus, if a company can arrange to give real problems to R & D to work on, the R & D effort can be effectively utilized. In a sense the management "trick" is to convince R & D that the conceptual market need, which has been identified, is the most intellectually challenging problem around. Then you must encourage the R & D people to work on that.

New product development should be directed at market requirements.

The second fallacy is rooted in the notion that adding a little bit of R & D effort will generally improve the new product development effort (at least until a point of diminishing returns is reached). I discuss this fallacy in the next section.

Optimizing Research and Development Spending

Several writers have reported on searches for an optimum research spending level. Such an optimum might be as illustrated in Figure 3-1. These searchers have reported correlations between the R & D spending levels and stock price, the price/earnings ratio, or return on sales. The reported correlations lead the various authors to conclude that there is an optimum R & D spending level, which maximizes profits, for instance.

There is no profit-maximizing R & D spending level.

In my view, searching for the optimum R & D spending level is rather like searching for an unidentified flying object, the Loch Ness monster, or the abominable snowman. It's fun to search and there are tantalizing clues that something may be found. However, unlike a search for (perhaps) mythical objects, there cannot actually be a profit-maximizing R & D spending level. The reasons for this fall into six categories.

Reductions in Current Profits

Increased R & D spending must reduce current year profits. This fact implies a negative rather than positive correlation, unless R & D could be performed at the beginning of the year and still produce later profits in the same year.

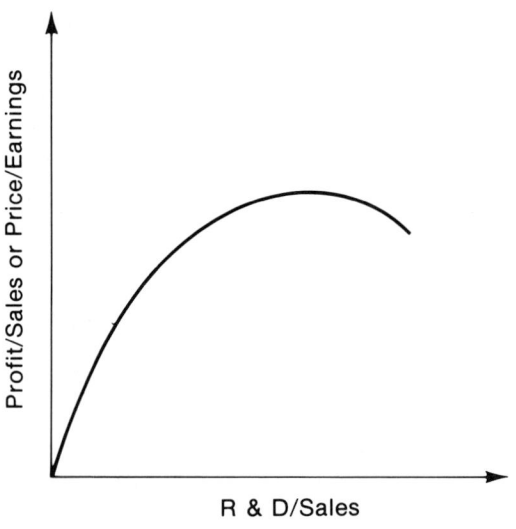

Figure 3-1. Finding an optimum R & D level

Financial Statement Strictures

Corporate financial statements, on which the data correlations are based, include R & D for a mix of current businesses and future business initiations. Typically, R & D is not related to current businesses but rather to future business initiations. Thus, R & D normally is not related to current earnings or stock prices in any direct way. At least one company has candidly acknowledged that half the company uses virtually no R & D. Consequently, the other half of the company has an R & D spending level that is effectively twice that reported for the entire company.

The payoff, if any, for an R & D program will be sometime in the future. Some payoffs occur quickly, and others not so quickly. Thus, an increase in R & D spending might be correlated with future profit increases. However, there will not be any specific number of years' delay in this effect because it clearly depends on the duration of the development program. Nevertheless, there might be periods that were typical of certain industries, for instance, three years in the scientific instrumentation field or twenty years in the photovoltaic energy field.

A further complication is that future profit depends on many investments in addition to R & D spending. Capital investments and staff upgrading are two investments that impact future company profit.

Beyond these issues, profits (current and future) are strongly affected by factors other than investment. The effective tax rate (which can be altered merely by the mix of domestic and foreign business), the management of inventory and accounts receivable, and competition all have a direct effect on profits.

Financial statements can present a misleading picture.

Irrational Factors

Stock prices and price/earnings ratios depend on many factors, some of which are purely emotional. The gyrations in some stock prices (Polaroid, for instance, in the late 1970s) clearly illustrate a lack of correlation with R & D spending (as a percentage of sales). Sometimes there may be a big increase in the ratio for R & D to sales, which can occur because company sales evaporate, and this should depress rather than increase the stock price.

Uneven Work Flow

All managers, including R & D managers, try to avoid rapid increases or decreases in department staff. The former consumes too much effort in recruiting and orienting new personnel; the latter leads to reduced morale. Thus, unless the R & D group has a stockpile of equally worthy projects to initiate, the effectiveness of the R & D effort must tend to vary with time. Rather than fire R & D personnel when high payoff projects are concluded, the R & D manager allows personnel to work on lower or marginal projects.

Loosely Defined Categories

What a company reports as its R & D expenditure is usually a mix of many things. For instance, it is not unusual to find technical service work (maintenance or modifications to an existing product) performed by R & D personnel being reported as R & D. But there is no real way this "R & D" can lead to innovative new products, although it may indeed be an expeditious way to help current year profits.

Cause-Effect

Correlations do not establish cause. More profitable companies may spend more on R & D because they have the money to spend.

Do not search for an optimum; spend as much as the market justifies.

There appears to be a better approach than to search through numerical data for a relationship to try to establish an optimum R & D spending level. The best course is to spend as much as possible on need or market directed R & D where the prospective returns promise to be greater than returns from alternative investments. Within this guideline, R & D spending must be limited by its impact on current year profits and moderated by staffing levels.

HIGHLIGHTS Profitable new product development requires (1) a strategic framework, (2) a market idea or concept, (3) an innovative idea for a product to satisfy that market need, (4) a profit plan, and (5) teamwork.

Success is never guaranteed; so good management concentrates limited resources on a small number of potential winners.

New product development ideas should arise from a marketing need or opportunity rather than from a technical interest or capability.

FURTHER READING

Booz, Allen & Hamilton Consulting Company. "Management of New Products." New York: Booz, Allen & Hamilton, 1968. A portion of this is reprinted as chap. 14, pp. 177–187, in R. R. Rothberg, ed., *Corporate Strategy and Product Innovation*, 2nd ed. New York: Free Press, 1981.
   This is a succinct review of success rates and the need for market, rather than R & D, leadership.

G. Coggshall. "Currency Inspected at Rates of 192,000 Notes/Hr." *Industrial Research & Development*, November 1981, pp. 122–125.
   This is a description of the currency inspection system.

R. G. Cooper. "How to Identify Potential New Product Winners." *Research Management*, September 1980, pp. 10–19.
   Fifteen factors that make the difference between success and failure are identified.

C. M. Crawford. "New Product Failure Rates—Facts and Fallacies." *Research Management*, September 1979, pp. 9–13.
   Crawford points out methodological problems with success-failure studies and argues that success is more likely than is generally reported.

C. D. Fogg. "The Market-Directed Product Development Process." *Research Management*, September 1977, pp. 25–32.
   This is a review of how to inject market guidance and avoid pitfalls of R & D guidance of product development.

E. A. Gee and C. Tyler. "Managing Research for Profitable Innovation." Chap. 13, pp. 208–221, in E. A. Gee and C. Tyler, *Managing Innovation*. New York: Wiley-Interscience, 1976.
   How to fit management of the R & D function into the corporation's strategic framework is the subject of this chapter.

R. W. James. "Decision Points in Developing New Products." Small Business Management Series No. 39. Washington, D. C.: Small Business Administration, 1976.
   This excellent short booklet emphasizes market direction to new product development.

D. G. Marquis. "The Anatomy of Successful Innovations." Chap. 2, pp. 14–25, in R. R. Rothberg, ed., *Corporate Strategy and Product Innovation*, 2nd ed. New York: Free Press, 1981.
   Marquis lists characteristics of successful innovations.

B. S. Old. "Corporate Directors Should Rethink Technology." *Harvard Business Review*, January–February 1982, pp. 6–14.

> This is a report on the correlation of technology investment (R & D plus new plant and equipment) with corporate growth.

W. E. Souder and A. K. Chakrabarti. "Industrial Innovation: A Demographical Analysis." *IEEE Transactions on Engineering Management*, vol. EM-26, no. 4 (November 1979), pp. 101–109.
> This is a study of 116 innovations, looking at factors leading to success or failure.

B. Twiss. *Managing Technological Innovation*, 2nd ed. London: Longman, 1980.
> Twiss covers how to manage the R & D operation.

W. D. Zarecor. "High-Technology Product Planning." *Harvard Business Review*, January–February 1975, pp. 108–115.
> How to develop further products after the first product gets your company off to a good start is the topic of this article.

Part 2

THE MARKET

After strategy, the next most crucial factor is the existence of a market need. A problem idea has to be created or recognized. You have to identify what the market need is or will be. Successful new products fill some need, even if it is only a created one. First I review how to identify such needs (Chapter 4). Then I describe how to gather detailed information about product attributes that will allow you to develop a winning product (Chapter 5).

Part 2

4

Market Need

KEY POINTS

Problem ideas at which you should direct your new product development effort come from the market.

Inherent needs provide the best opportunity for success in new product development.

Postulated needs are another source of opportunity.

Never undertake new product development without market guidance.

There are five techniques R & D personnel can use to understand potential markets.

INHERENT NEEDS

Inherent needs, those which are clear and not satisfied, represent the best opportunity for successful new product development. As an example, there is an inherent need for shoplifting prevention. If a store is losing goods worth $10,000 per month, a system to prevent shoplifting that sells for $60,000 would have a half-year payback. Therefore, that would be an attractive product to the store. Conversely, if the system cost the store $1 million, it is unlikely the store would be interested because eliminating the shoplifting losses totally would not pay for the product in a reasonable period of time.

There are other examples of inherent needs that one can easily imagine. For instance, better thermal insulation is something for which there is an inherent need. That is a need that will grow, in fact, as the cost of energy increases.

In 1850, when Levi Strauss went west during the California gold rush, he believed that the inherent need was canvas tents to house the miners. However, Levi Strauss met a disgruntled miner who wanted a sturdy pair of pants that could withstand the rigors of digging. Thus, he recognized that the inherent need was in fact different than his original perception. He used some of his tent canvas to make a pair of pants for the miner. He went on from there to found what is today one of the largest and most successful consumer goods clothing businesses in the world.

When an inherent need can be identified, it normally provides the best opportunity for successful new product development.

How can you find inherent needs? Where do you look for problem ideas? In general, you should look to the outside world:

- Is there a way to reduce a customer's cost?
- Will changing regulations create a new requirement?
- Is there a better way to meet a customer's needs?
- Can you provide a customer with better quality?

Keep asking these questions of yourself and sometime you will develop a notion. That notion may be the germ of a successful new product. The currency scanner discussed in Chapter 3 is an example of this questioning process.

A DuPont product, Starblast, filled an unlikely inherent need—it replaced sand—by saving money. Sand itself is cheap, but when it is used for sandblasting, to prepare a metal surface for painting, the total process also requires labor. The quality of the subsequent paint job depends on the uniformity of the abrading job done by the sandblasting. DuPont created Starblast, which cost about four times more than sand but did a better job in less time (hence a labor saving) with a smaller volume of abrasive and reduced levels of dust.

There are ways of making needs come to you.

You can also encourage needs to find you. For instance, Wang Laboratories holds an annual conference for users of their word processors. In 1978, users proposed an optional automatic envelope feeder and addresser. Wang successfully introduced this a year later. Proctor & Gamble (and other companies) maintain toll-free telephone numbers so customers can easily call them. This approach can expose a product shortfall, which can then stimulate a better new product development effort.

POSTULATED NEEDS

There are two sorts of postulated needs to which companies occasionally respond. The first is the existence of a very large market. The problem here is the market share fallacy. The second is a need derived from technological possibilities.

Market Share Fallacy

The market share fallacy is rooted in the assumption that where a very large market exists, it is possible to get significant sales volume by gaining only a very small percentage share. Only a small share would supposedly provide sufficient sales volume to be profitable. As an example, the United States market for new automobiles approximates ten million units a year. One percent of this market is a hundred thousand cars. One percent appears to be a very small number. If caught up in the market share fallacy, a person would say, "Gee, all we have to do is get 1 percent of that market and we've got a swell little business." The fallacy is that you cannot get 1 percent or even 0.1 percent of the market in this kind of a situation because you lack a dealer network and the infrastructure of spare parts supplies. In other situations you may have a product advocate who says they need only 5 percent of a market. This is their way of appearing conservative as a justification for a new product development effort. After all, 5 percent is a very small share. When this happens, you have to be skeptical and ask yourself is this plausible. Can we really get that share?

Do not justify new product development on the basis of requiring only a very small market share.

Needs Based on Technological Possibilities

Technical geniuses (and some people who are less than geniuses) frequently envision ways to create new products. They often devise novel approaches to exploit new technology. Frequently this merely leads to a solution looking for a problem and can be a very wasteful use of corporate resources.

A solution seeking a problem can waste money.

CASE HISTORIES

Structural Pressure-Sensitive Tape

In about 1978, the chief executives and founders of two innovative companies met. In many senses these men were the technical spark plugs and entrepreneurial geniuses of the two companies. One company led in the field of anaerobic (adhesive) chemicals, used principally for joining metal parts together. The second company led in pressure-sensitive tapes used for a variety of commercial and consumer applications. These two entrepreneurs envisioned the possibility of creating a "structural" pressure-sensitive adhesive tape. They hoped to provide the convenience of pressure-sensitive tapes combined with the strength of structural, anaerobic adhesive chemicals. They thought such a tape could be used, for instance, for joining metal parts and could replace spot welding or other metal joining operations in many applications.

They turned this concept over to the central research groups of each of the two corporations for development work. A year and a half later the work had progressed to the point where the program was then seen as having four phases: (1) Get something that worked, that is, demonstrate feasibility, (2) Develop a tough and reproducible product, (3) Get a product capable of filling gaps between the parts to be joined, (4) Develop a single-component product, that is, one that does not require a primer. Thus, after a year and a half of development work, it was clear that feasibility had not yet been demonstrated, such products as existed were not totally reproducible, such products as existed were not capable of filling gaps between components to be joined, and the product as it then existed required a primer (which in fact was a carcinogen).

Unfortunately, only at this point, a year and a half after technical development commenced, was market research undertaken. The market research effort required only a few months and cost only 10 percent of what had already been spent on R & D. It clearly established that none of the different kinds of joints that might be bonded were realistically amenable to structural pressure-sensitive tapes, even if such a product could be developed.

Market research is vital.

A lesson to be learned from this kind of effort is not that it should not have been started. Indeed, the effort should have been started. But a market research effort should have been undertaken within three to six months of the commencement of the technical development effort. Market research would have provided essential guidance about the key characteristics that had to be given attention during the development effort. Also, it would have highlighted that the technical development effort was not coming close to satisfying realistic market needs much earlier and at much less cost.

Pringle's Chips

Proctor & Gamble used its considerable engineering know-how to devise a way to convert potatoes into chips. The goal was a chip that would stay fresh longer, break less often, travel better, and use less shelf space. These attributes are important to a store supplier, which P & G is. The resulting chips were an engineering marvel, but the consumers' needs and tastes were not emphasized. It is believed that P & G losses on this product from 1968 to 1981 exceeded $200 million.

In this case the postulated need was partly correct and partly wrong. The attributes of importance to a store supplier did not turn out to be ones consumers valued—at least so far.

MARKET GUIDANCE FOR R & D EFFORTS

Everyone has heard of the R & D program that produced a "solution looking for a problem." When this happens, the company has incurred unnecessary expense, but, more important, has applied precious limited R & D resources to an effort that will not produce a profit. This observation does not imply that all R & D programs must have an immediate profit prospect.

Nevertheless, it would be a mistake for R & D or other technical personnel to presume that any new undertaking is justifiable because it has not been done before or because the marketing department requests it. When starting a fundamental project, one aimed only at obtaining knowledge, R & D may lack certainty about what has to be done, but the key managers must have some application scenario in mind. This sense of who might use the knowledge output is crucial. It indicates

Blindly initiating new product development without validated market guidance leads to disaster.

where to make inquiries about what is really important rather than merely intellectually challenging.

To put it differently, there are the right kind of risks and the wrong kind of risks to take. This section is concerned with helping R & D or other technical personnel sort out those risks so you can concentrate limited resources on programs that are more likely to be profitable. The key to this sorting out is to gain some (even if limited) understanding of the prospective market for the output of the R & D program—to see how the results will be applied in the real world. This process requires getting out of the laboratory environment, either actually or by proxy. Ultimately, there have to be users. An understanding of user needs is the key to successful R & D.

Understanding users' needs is essential.

There are five techniques R & D personnel can use to gain this vital understanding of potential markets: brainstorming, quick estimates, on-line information retrieval, dyad teams, and market research.

Brainstorming

Brainstorming is a creative process that is used to produce ideas, such as ideas for new products. Although it is more often used to generate solution ideas, brainstorming is also important in generating problem ideas, for two disparate reasons. In some cases there may be a strong desire for a new product development effort but no promising idea. In such a situation brainstorming may well produce a promising lead. In other cases there may already be an idea, but also uncertainty about its promise. In either case brainstorming is a useful initial effort.

Multiple points of view are a useful screen.

Brainstorming helps provide market guidance because it involves several people giving several points of view. The old adage about two heads being better than one proves itself true repeatedly. Drawing upon the experience of several people, the brainstorming process helps assure that a candidate R & D program is market related and not misdirected. If marketing or other people with an external orientation participate, it is even more likely to be effective. I discuss the techniques for brainstorming in Part 3.

Brainstorming draws only upon participants' knowledge. As such, the process may depend more on opinions than objective market data. Thus, one of four methods must always be used in conjunction with brainstorming: quick estimates, on-line information retrieval, dyad teams, and market research.

Quick Estimates

The quick estimates approach might also be called the "back of the envelope" method because that is all that is required to test the reasonableness of the program justification. Basically, one simply applies general knowledge to judge if a proposed effort is worthy.

In 1976, a senior researcher proposed a $100,000 development program to formulate a new compound for use in one aspect of car manufacturing. As R & D programs went in this particular company, this was a moderately large program. But it certainly was not so large as to be considered a major expenditure program. For illustration (and to conceal the specifics), let me pretend that this compound would be used to produce cabling insulation, that the selling price of comparable compounds was $3 per thousand feet of cabling used, and that each car would use about thirty-five feet of this cabling. In this case the general knowledge that we draw upon is the fact that about ten million cars are manufactured in the United States each year. Therefore, if the company could capture 100 percent of the market, the annual sales would approximate $1,000,000. Consequently, the before-tax profits (assuming the resultant product was about as profitable as other company products) would approximate $100,000 per year. Based on other products sold to this market, only a 10 percent market share was realistic—if the development was successful. Thus, the company was faced with the certain expenditure of $100,000 and the uncertain prospect of earning $10,000 per year. Such a program is clearly not an attractive undertaking as proposed and must be abandoned or redirected.

In many instances you can easily and quickly estimate market size and judge whether to authorize an initial effort. It is frequently desirable to authorize one, three, or six months of initial work. The goal of this short period is to learn enough to decide if more effort is justified. When this approach is used, there must be both market analysis and technical development work done during this initial period.

A quick estimate is cheap and always a useful check.

Sometimes a new product development program should be allowed a short trial period to develop enough information to decide whether continuation is justified.

On-Line Information Retrieval

Today there is an almost astronomical amount of data available through *on-line information retrieval* services. These services include Lockheed Dialog and SDC Search Service. They can be accessed by use of a suitable terminal and telephonic connection. The costs are sufficiently low so that the small company can overcome the comparative advantage that the large company usually enjoys.

In early 1981, I wanted to learn about recent developments in ultraviolet curing. In somewhat less than an hour and at a cost less than $100, I searched the dozen most likely data bases in Lockheed Dialog. I learned that there were about twenty-five hundred citations that met my indexing criteria. These were among the nearly five million abstracted documents on file in these dozen data bases. For the few most relevant of the citations I ordered either abstracts or the full original document by mail. Within days of initiating my inquiry I was able to review what was recently published in the area of interest.

It is cheap to check the published background information.

This kind of background checking has its limitations, but it provides two valuable aids. First, it may uncover the fact that someone else has already done what you are contemplating. Second, it will indicate sources of further information about the market. By identifying societies, associations, journal editors, companies, and others involved in the market, you learn who to interview directly to gain firsthand information.

Dyad Teams

Dyads that put a company in touch with the real world are invaluable.

A dyad is two people, and a *dyad team* is two people working as a team. In the context of this discussion, such a team would normally consist of one person from R & D and one person from marketing. Such a team would call on prospective customers and users to learn about their problems, thus gaining direct market input on real market needs. In some cases a *triad team*, with a manufacturing person added, might be appropriate.

In 1977, in one use of such an approach, one team quickly learned that the idea they were hoping to exploit had already been considered (and dropped) by a much bigger competitor. The other company had quit about eighteen months previously. The dyad team realized that something might be amiss. Further searching for a market failed to turn up any significant possibility commensurate with the development cost.

A further benefit of R & D/marketing dyad teams is the harmony these can promote between the two departments, which are often antagonistic. I explore this issue at greater length in Part 5.

Market Research

Should you use an outside consulting organization to conduct market research about a contemplated idea? Your own dyad team can also conduct market research, as can your marketing, sales, or R & D department, but outsiders bring an objectivity that no group of employees can ever match. Further, the outside firm can keep your company's name confidential, which may be an important competitive advantage. Such firms can frequently conduct such an assignment more quickly and economically than the concerned company. Often the consultant already knows where to start, what to do, and how to do it. I discuss market research in the next chapter.

At some point formal market research is always required.

HIGHLIGHTS

Efforts aimed at filling unfilled inherent needs are the best opportunity for new product development.

New product development efforts aimed at postulated needs, especially those that are untested against market reality, are usually unsuccessful.

Four ways to test the market are brainstorming, quick estimates, on-line information retrieval, and dyad teams.

Formal market research is always required at some point.

FURTHER READING

L. Adler. "New Ways to Identify Business Opportunities." *Industrial Marketing Management*, vol. 6 (November 1977), pp. 404–409.
   This provocative article proposes a nine-step systems approach to replace the haphazard method frequently used.

G. Binetti. "On-Line Information Retrieval Aids New Product Development." *Industrial Marketing Management*, vol. 9 (July 1980), pp. 247–251.
   Here are some examples of how on-line information retrieval can help.

P. M. Chisnall. "Management of Innovation." Chap. 10, pp. 207–237, in P. M. Chisnall, *Effective Industrial Marketing*. London: Longman, 1977.
The need for market direction is the subject of this chapter.

A. Gruber. "The Marketing Manager's Guide to New Product Invention." New York: AMACOM, 1977.
This short booklet advises what to do to find and recognize ideas.

R. E. Herzog. "The Link Between Customer and Engineer." *Machine Design*, July 11, 1974, pp. 113–116.
Herzog stresses the need for engineers to check the market before they go too far.

D. S. Hopkins. *The Marketing Plan.* Conference Board report 801. New York: Conference Board, 1981.
This excellent report covers the role and structure of a formal market plan.

L. Ingrassia. "Taking Chances: How Four Companies Spawn New Products by Encouraging Risks." *The Wall Street Journal*, September 18, 1980.
This is a news article about Texas Instruments, Wang, and two others.

P. Kotler. "New-Product Decisions." Chap. 13, pp. 464–513, in P. Kotler, *Marketing Management*, 2nd ed. Englewood Cliffs, N.J.: Prentice-Hall, 1972.
This college text presents a very good overview.

J. Murphy. "The 'Starblast' Alternative." *DuPont Magazine*, July–August 1977, pp. 7–9. See also *DuPont Magazine*, March–April 1982, p. 29.
The Starblast story is the subject of the first citation, and a bit more information is provided in the second citation.

D. E. New and J. L. Schlachter. "Abandon Bad R & D Projects with Earlier Marketing Appraisals." *Industrial Marketing Management*, vol. 8 (November 1979), pp. 274–280.
These authors stress need to involve marketing at an early point.

G.L.M. Quintelier. "A Technique for Problem Finding and Market Introduction." *Research Management*, September 1978, pp. 26–28.
Quintelier proposes the use of "problem scouts" to find existing market needs.

K. H. Vesper. "New-Venture Ideas: Do Not Overlook Experience

Factor." *Harvard Business Review*, July–August 1979, pp. 164–170.
> *Vesper has a good list of idea sources on page 166.*

E. von Hippel. "Get New Products from Customers." *Harvard Business Review*, March–April 1982, pp. 117–122.
> *How to get new product ideas from customers is the topic of this article.*

W. White. "The Research Survey—A Way to Bridge the Gap Between Lab and Market." *Research Management*, July 1978, pp. 14–18.
> *White proposes that researchers conduct some market research.*

5

Market Research

KEY POINTS Although not infallible, market research is vital to new product development.

There are four questions market research must answer.

Market research can be conducted by company personnel or by an outside firm. Each approach has advantages.

There are four main methods for conducting market research.

BASIC ISSUES

Market research is essential to new product development. It is the means by which a company attempts to identify what is going to happen in the future. To be effective, market research must clearly recognize that the future is uncertain. A purpose of market research is to reduce that uncertainty, even though it can never eliminate it.

The future is uncertain.

Market surveys are typically done six months to several years prior to the product being available. The sampled attitude may change. You are therefore betting that external conditions will not be altered dramatically by the time the product is available. There is always the issue of bias when market research is being conducted. The bias is on the part of both the interviewer and the respondent. Market research takes time, especially if it is to be done well. After it has been done, there has to be time available to react to the findings. If you are unwilling or unable to react to these findings, then there is certainly no point in conducting the market research.

It is particularly difficult to engage in market research where the markets you are looking at are changing very rapidly. The market requirements today will not govern the market when the product development program is complete. That is, there is a "moving target" problem, and you have to anticipate what the market will be at the time of product introduction. This is the same problem a bird hunter faces when aiming at a bird. The hunter must aim ahead of the bird to get the shot where the bird will be when the shot arrives.

To put it another way, market research is not infallible, and one must not be deluded by its results. However, when market research is reasonably conducted, it should provide a good clue. It will normally reveal whether there will be, in fact, a market need and how large it will be.

Although imperfect, market research is essential to new product development.

CASE HISTORY

In 1980, the R & D department of a company conceived of a very novel low-cost way to perform a function that was done at that time by a $5,000 device. They believed they could produce their novel device at a cost permitting them to sell it for $4,000. Their product, although technically novel, would be functionally similar to the existing $5,000 device. Thus, the basis of product differentiation would be primarily price.

The R & D department wanted $50,000 to build a prototype of the device. Senior corporate management decided first to have a consulting market research effort to decide whether the $50,000 expenditure was justified. The market research effort was estimated to cost $5,000 and could be thought of as an insurance policy premium on the proposed $50,000 expense.

During the first month of what was proposed as a three-month market research assignment, a market researcher was able to identify three other functionally equivalent devices. These were already selling at prices of $2,000, $1,000, and $700, respectively. As a result of this discovery, the market researcher recommended that the effort be abandoned immediately. Further, he recommended that the market research effort be stopped at the end of one rather than three months, at a much lower cost to the company. In this case we see how a very brief examination of the outside world revealed that a proposed new product development effort would have been completely wasted.

CRUCIAL MARKET RESEARCH ISSUES

There are four crucial questions market research should answer.

There are four crucial issues in market research. First, it must be established that the product concept is actually functionally adequate. Does it do the job it is intended to do? Assuming that this can be established, the next question is whether it offers any performance advantages. How is it better than alternative ways to accomplish the function? Does it do something better or faster? Most significantly, is that performance advantage important to the prospective user?

The third issue is whether prospective buyers have some economic incentive to buy the new product. Here you have to divide the world into two classes of people:

1. Those already performing the function and who have some equipment on hand to do it. This existing equipment would have to be displaced by your proposed equipment.
2. Those who might be buyers who do not have any equipment yet. These people are much easier prospective targets to sell your equipment to. They do not have a vested stake in equipment or operator training.

The fourth issue is to decide whether the business one can obtain as a result of the new product development effort will be sufficiently large and profitable. Another way to look at these last two issues is from the point of view of acceptable financial return. Both buyer and manufacturer have to exceed minimum acceptable financial terms for the effort to be an attractive proposition.

CASE HISTORY

In 1979, a company that manufactured and sold a sophisticated $100,000 microdensitometer to astronomical observatories and film manufacturers (to evaluate photographic images) was confronted with an opportunity. The opportunity arose when a brilliant senior engineer conceived of a modification to the microdensitometer that would permit it to perform a particular photogrammetric production task with very high resolution. (The microdensitometer worked by measuring film transmission point by point with very great accuracy. This task was one the photogrammetric users also had, although the way they would manipulate the data differed from that of an astronomical observatory or a film manufacturer.) The brilliant senior engineer had even found a leading supplier of photogrammetric equipment who was excited about the idea. The engineer had requested $150,000 to build a prototype instrument.

The market for photogrammetric instruments was unfamiliar to the microdensitometer company. Senior management turned to an outside marketing consultant to decide if there was really a market for this particular instrument. The marketing consultant used direct and telephone interviews to get answers to these four questions:

1. Is the product concept *functionally suitable?*
2. Does it offer *performance advantages?*
3. Is there an *economic incentive* for buyers to switch?
4. Is available business *attractive to us?*

It did not take very long to discover that the proposed instrument was not entirely suitable functionally. The consultant uncovered this despite the fact that the prospective manufacturer had conducted a thorough technical review with technical experts. The consultant discovered that there were certain photogrammetric situations with which the proposed instrument could not deal. The market was thus smaller than the client originally expected.

The second major finding was that photogrammetric companies were only marginally interested in the very high resolution performance that this instrument offered. What they really wanted was a very low cost means of accomplishing the function. The instrument as envisioned was going to sell for approximately $500,000. With one exception all the interviewed photogrammetric companies were interested in spending perhaps $50,000 to perform the function. To put it differently, what the client perceived to be a performance advantage (high resolution) was not perceived by prospective customers to be as important as low cost. That is, they could simply avoid performing the function entirely and leave the task undone. As a result of these two findings, the market research consultant could validate for the company that there was indeed a problem. However, the high-resolution approach to solving it was not desired in the marketplace. The consultant recommended that the effort be redirected to devising a low-cost solution to the basic photogrammetric problem.

Multiattribute Utility Analysis

Multiattribute utility analysis (MUA), also called *conjoint analysis*, is a useful technique to employ when trying to answer the second and third of the four crucial market research questions. MUA can provide a quantitative measure of the performance advantage your product has for a prospective user. MUA can also estimate what price the product will command for a particular combination of attributes.

Use MUA to answer the second and third market research questions.

MUA individually asks prospective users to rank a series of cards. Each card lists a group of product attributes and values for those attributes, as illustrated in Table 5-1. In actual practice, some or all of the attribute values might be numerical rather than qualitative. The respondent is given a group of cards (perhaps one or two dozen), as shown in Figure 5-1. One card has the most attractive combination of product attributes (bottom right in Figure 5-1), and one card has the least attractive combination (upper left in Figure 5-1). Other cards have

TABLE 5-1 Hypothetical Attributes and Values for Multiattribute Utility Analysis

Attribute	Values			
Price	High	Medium	Low	
Speed	Low	Medium	High	
Features	One	Few	Several	Many
Warranty	None	Limited	Full	

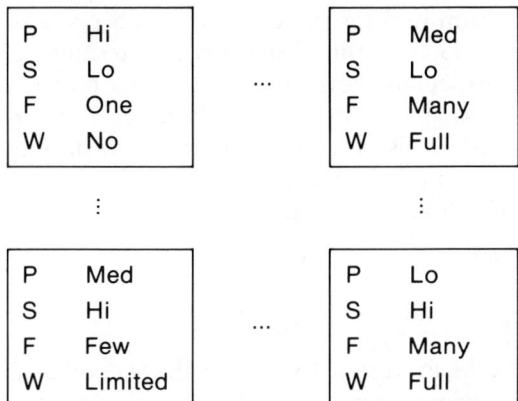

Figure 5-1. Some of the cards with combinations of product attributes to be ranked by a respondent for a multiattribute utility analysis

random combinations. The respondent is asked to rank all the cards.

Then the data for a group of respondents are analyzed with a suitable computer analysis. Basically, the goal is to assign a set of scalar values to each attribute's values so that the total utility for each combination provides a best fit with the respondents' rankings. The outcome is a series of scalar plots indicating the relative utility for each value of each attribute (Figure 5-2). In the illustrated case we see that there is little

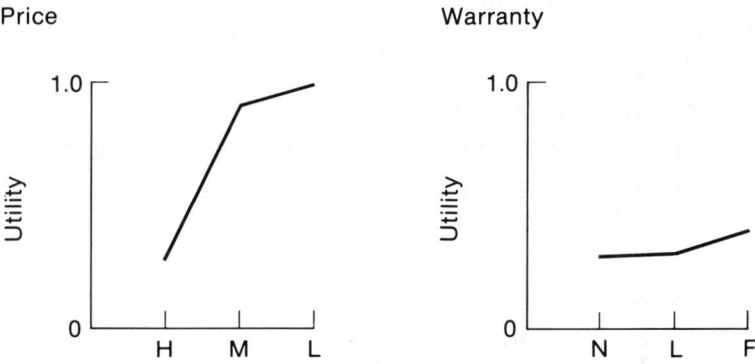

Figure 5-2. Some of the results for a multiattribute utility analysis

difference between medium and low price, but a high price is perceived to have much lower utility. Similarly, warranty is relatively unimportant, especially compared to offering a product with a medium or low price. MUA not only helps answer market research questions, it also provides guidance for design engineers by showing which product attributes should be given serious attention and which are less important.

MUA also assists design engineers.

Focus Groups

Focus groups can also be used to help answer the second and third questions. A focus group usually consists of six to twelve current or prospective users of the product. Normally, focus groups are used for consumer products, but they can also be used for industrial products. Frequently, a product model or prototype, often without company identification, is demonstrated to this small group. Their reactions to preplanned questions are recorded on audio- or videotape. Proper conduct of a focus group is difficult, so they are usually run by consulting specialists. The goal is to gather qualitative information about user opinions, buying or usage patterns, product features or attributes, brand identifications, and similar factors.

Focus groups help answer the second and third market research questions.

Timing

Market research must also estimate how rapidly the market will develop. If there is an inherent need, sales growth may be quick or limited only by production capacity. If your product concept is very innovative, it may require many years. In the latter case five factors appear to govern how quickly sales will develop:

1. Compatibility (the degree to which the product is in harmony with the user's existing values and experiences)
2. Complexity (the degree to which the product concept can be understood and eventually used)
3. Divisibility (the degree to which the product can be tested or sampled on a limited basis)
4. Communicability (the degree to which product utility can be explained to potential users)
5. Relative advantage (the degree to which the new product is truly superior to alternative ways to deal with the problem)

There are no analytic schemes that accurately predict how quickly a market will develop. Thus, you must rely on your judgment about how your innovative product compares to others for which historical data are available.

Your judgment is essential in estimating how quickly the market will develop.

PERFORMANCE OF MARKET RESEARCH

There are two basic approaches to conducting market research. The first is to do it with your own company personnel; the second is to use outsiders, typically market research consultants. Company personnel start out with a greater familiarity with the company and presumably of the product concept being considered. If they work on this, they will learn as a result of engaging in a new experience. A dyad of marketing and R & D or engineering personnel can help build bridges between these departments within a company. This approach often works well in conducting market research for a new product concept.

Outsiders can bring a degree of objectivity to the examination that company personnel could never match. In general, outside consultants will also have a broad outlook. They will have done a lot of market research for a variety of products. Thus, they will have relevant experience on the techniques of doing market research. When outsiders are used, the company identity can be concealed, which often provides an essential competitive advantage.

Market research performed by outside consultants is usually more objective.

New product development failures often result from the failure to conduct market research or from conducting market research inappropriately. For instance, a major pitfall is to describe a new product concept to a prospective buyer and ask whether he or she wants it. At this point it costs the prospective buyer absolutely nothing to say yes. In fact, in general, they will do so for two reasons. First, they would rather avoid a confrontation or disappointment with the person who is interviewing them. Second, because it costs them nothing to let the development proceed, they are willing to be encouraging. They can even hope that the development will in fact lead to something successful, even if it seems doubtful.

The goal of market research is to learn, not to sell the product. Asking whether a customer wants it is therefore maladaptive. The kind of questions that market researchers should be asking are aimed at finding out how the function is performed now. They want to learn all the details. Then it is important to

The goal of market research is to learn about the market, not to sell the idea.

find out what the cost elements and trends are. This is part of anticipating the moving target and trying to project. The goal is to anticipate what the cost structure will be in the prospective buyer's company.

When conducting market research about some product concept, it is also important to try to learn what aspects the prospective buyer considers most in need of improvement. It may be that the product concept is miscast and that some other related development would be much more valuable. This was the case with the photogrammetric instrument. It is also important to try to anticipate what competition there might be. Competition can be determined by asking whether someone else has attempted improvements or is believed to be at work on improvements within the product concept area. Occasionally, this will reveal that there is a need, but you are one or two years behind others in developing a solution to the problem. Finally, it is important to get an estimate of what the proposed new product would be worth to the buyer financially. The answers to this serve as a check on the prior questions.

CASE HISTORY

In 1976, one company was offered a license to manufacture a product called Z-tape, which was a plastic product somewhat comparable to velcro. Figure 5-3 is a hasty survey of prospective buyers company personnel conducted. Interviews were conducted both in person and by telephone, in general asking the questions on the questionnaire. The broad product concept was to sell the Z-tape at a price somewhat less than that of velcro. The first thing that was learned was that the velcro market was of the order of $15 million a year, which meant that the Z-tape market was, at the most, less than that, probably about $12 million a year if 100 percent of the market could be shifted away from velcro to Z-tape. The second thing that was learned was that there were no velcro users for whom a small cost saving (prospectively a 20 percent cost reduction) was very important. That saving could not justify shifting from a proven to an unproven product. The third and most surprising finding was that another company had conducted the same market research two years earlier. The other, much larger, company had not gone ahead with the project. Thus, their much

Figure 5-3. Survey questionnaire for Z-tape field research

Company_____ Persons interviewed_____
Address_____ _____
City_____ Product discussed_____
Product (lines)_____ Interviewer_____
Market_____ Date_____

A. Questions (not verbatim) asked the interviewee.
   - Describe your present reclosure or refastening method.
   - What advantages does it offer over other methods you have used or considered?

     East to use _____   Traditional   _____   Durability _____
     Low cost   _____   Versatile   _____   Other   _____
     Reliable   _____   Easy to install _____

   - What special conditions or considerations that affect its closure or fastener are applicable to your product?

     Exposure   _____   Customer profile _____
     Reclosure life _____   Environment   _____
     Aesthetics   _____   Other   _____

   - What special equipment or human expertise is required in attaching the fastener to your product?
   - What do you consider to be the most important closure characteristic for your type of product?

     Ease of use   _____   Durability   _____
     Fashion/style _____   Versatility   _____
     Economics   _____   Industry similarity _____
     Reliability   _____   Other   _____

B. (Interviewer now shows, demonstrates, and explains the Z-Tape product, allowing the individual to "play with it.")
   - Have you ever seen a product like this before? If yes, what was your reaction to it?
   - What advantages do you see Z-Tape offering your product? Any disadvantages?
   - Which of the Z-Tape features might offer you an edge for your product in the marketplace?
   - Are there any modifications to Z-Tape that would be beneficial to your product?
   - Where would you expect this product to be priced, dollarwise? (Interviewer discloses cost and rate information)
   - How does that compare with the cost of your present system?

     Higher by_____   Cost of present
     Lower by_____   method_____

   - What actions would be required to get Z-Tape tested and evaluated for your product, and how much time usually is involved in such activities?

     Laboratory tests   _____   _____(Time)
     Product experimentation   _____   _____ ″
     FDA approval   _____   _____

Figure 5-3. Survey questionnaire for Z-tape field research (cont.)

    User panel trials   _____   _____
    Market tests   _____   _____
    Product specification _____   _____
    Total time   _____

- What additional information would you like to see about Z-Tape?

C. Postinterview interpretations (Interviewer asks himself or herself)
- On a scale of 1 to 10 (10 being highest fit possible) how would you judge the fit of Z-Tape in this industry with this product?
- What are the main obstacles to overcome? (Prioritize obstacles.)
- How does the cost issue look compared to other systems? Can higher costs be overcome by product superiority? Can lower costs be recognized as a clear-cut benefit?
- Who are the influentials (what positions) who must be "reached" in presenting and selling Z-Tape at this company?
- Where would you estimate the interest level? (1–10, with 10 being highest interest)

larger and more intensive market research effort must have indicated that the market would not justify Z-tape. As a result of this small amount of market research, the option to take out a license on Z-tape, at a cost of $1 million, was dropped.

MARKET RESEARCH METHODS

Data base searching is the best way to commence market research.

There are four principal market research methods. *Data base searching,* in which secondary sources of data are examined, is always a good way to start market research. On-line information retrieval, discussed in the previous chapter, is one way to do this. It is quick and cheap, but, because it is indirect and limited to published information, it has its limitations. Nevertheless, a search using the *standard industrial classification (SIC) codes* may quickly pinpoint data about a target industry. This can then be used to direct the other three methods of market research. A patent search can also be done, and this is almost always significant.

The other three methods, *personal interviews, mailed questionnaires,* and *telephone interviews,* have the advantage of putting the market researcher, whether company personnel or

TABLE 5-2 Use of SIC Code Sample to Estimate Potential for New Lens Grinding Equipment

SIC Code	Company Annual Sales ($ Millions)	Number of Companies	Existing Lens Grinders per Company	Market Potential (Units)
3811—Engineering & Scientific Instruments	<10	120	0.7	84
	10–100	40	1.3	52
	100–500	10	3.2	32
	>500	4	7.9	32
3832—Optical Instruments and Lenses	<10	90	4.6	414
	10–100	30	20	600
	100–500	8	43	344
	>500	2	68	136
3851—Ophthalmic Goods	<10	200	7	1400
	10–100	20	23	460
	100–500	2	47	94
	>500	1	55	55

outside consultants, in direct contact with the outside world. People to be interviewed may include prospective purchasers, competitors, trade associations, trade publications, professional associations, industry consultants, university researchers, regulatory groups, component suppliers, and other people directly involved in the marketplace or technology.

Select the prospective purchasers to be representative of the various classes. For instance, if your product is a new attachment to a machine used to grind lenses, you might target the market to be instrument and ophthalmic goods manufacturers. In these businesses you might further segment between small, medium, and large companies, as illustrated in Table 5-2. You can determine the number of companies in each segment from industry surveys, census data, or on-line information retrieval from a suitable data base. Then you can interview a number of companies in each category to determine how many lens grinders are now in use. (In this case twelve categories have been used.) You can now estimate the potential sales for your product.

Market research performed by outside consultants is usually more objective.

The personal interview is the most effective market research method. It is flexible and permits thorough exploration of unexpected issues. However, whenever two people meet you run the risk of personal bias. The people may like each other and get along well, and everything looks rosy; or the people for some reason may have inappropriate personal chemistry. Then the interview turns out to be a disaster in some way or other. Face-to-face interviews are inevitably expensive, but in general the expense is justified if the stakes are high.

Market research by mail permits contacting a very large number of people, but it can take a long time. There is a bias in the nature of the people who respond—usually people with time or interest, who are not necessarily buyers or decision makers. And, of course, the total response is usually a small fraction of the people who have been sampled.

The telephone survey is somewhat of a compromise between face-to-face interviews and the use of a mail survey. It is possible to contact a fairly large number of people at reasonable cost. However, only a limited amount of information can be gleaned. Thus, the telephone interview, in common with the mail interview, lacks the direct exposure to the real situation.

HIGHLIGHTS Market research is essential to successful new product development.

There are four crucial issues in market research:

1. Is the product concept functionally suitable?
2. Does the product perform better than current products?
3. Is there an economic incentive for buyers to change products?
4. Is the available business attractive to us?

Multiattribute utility analysis and focus groups are two methods for answering the second and third questions.

Compatibility, complexity, divisibility, communicability, and relative advantage govern how quickly sales will develop.

Although market research can be performed by either company personnel or an outside firm, the latter are invariably more objective.

The four principal market research methods are data base searching (the best way to start), personal interviews, mailed questionnaires, and telephone interviews.

FURTHER READING

A. Bisio and L. E. Gastwirt. "Assessing Market Potential." *Research Management*, September 1981, pp. 18–22.
   A way to assess marketplace risks and costs is the subject of this article.

P. M. Chisnall. "Techniques of Market Research." Chap. 6, pp. 103–122, in P. M. Chisnall, *Effective Industrial Marketing*. London: Longman, 1977.
   This chapter is specific to the United Kingdom.

D. W. Collier. "The Creative Link Between Market and Technology." *Chemtech*, February 1975, pp. 90–93.
   Collier stresses the necessity of understanding user requirements.

D. W. Cowell and K. J. Blois. "Conducting Market Research for High Technology Products." *Industrial Marketing Management*, vol. 6 (October 1977), pp. 329–336.
   This article discusses three case histories.

W. E. Cox, Jr. *Industrial Marketing Research*. New York: Ronald Press, 1979.
   This is an excellent book.

J. J. Gilman. "Market Penetration Rates and Their Effect on Value." *Research Management*, March 1982, pp. 34–39.
   Gilman presents data showing how long it takes for innovative products to gain access to the market.

P. E. Green and Y. Wind. "New Way to Measure Consumer's Judgments." *Harvard Business Review*, July–August 1975, pp. 107–117. Chap. 22, pp. 273–289, in R. R. Rothberg, ed., *Corporate Strategy and Product Innovation*, 2nd ed. New York: Free Press, 1981.
   This is a thorough description of multiattribute utility analysis.

K. Holt. "Need Assessment in Product Innovation." *Research Management*, July 1976, pp. 24–28.
> Holt discusses the necessity of studying user and market needs.

P. Kotler. "Market Measurement and Forecasting." Chap. 7, pp. 192–225, in P. Kotler, *Marketing Management*, 2nd ed. Englewood Cliffs, N.J.: Prentice-Hall, 1972.
> Although in a book intended as a college text, this is a useful chapter.

A. T. Kruzas and R. C. Thomas. *Business Organizations and Agencies Directory.* Detroit: Gale Research, 1980.
> Section 22, pages 725–753, is a listing of data banks and computerized services.

T. Levitt. "The New Markets—Think Before You Leap." *Harvard Business Review*, May–June 1969, pp. 53–67.
> This classic article stresses the need for lots of careful thought.

M. B. McDonald, Jr. "Estimating Market Potential." Chap. 27, pp. 332–353, in R. R. Rothberg, ed., *Corporate Strategy and Product Innovation*, 2nd ed. New York: Free Press, 1981.
> McDonald provides sources of information to use for industrial markets.

A. Parasuraman. "Marketing Research by a Small Industrial Firm: A Case Study." *Industrial Marketing Management*, vol. 7 (August 1978), pp. 238–242.
> Parasuraman emphasizes the need for market research.

R. A. Peterson and R. A. Kerin. "The Effective Use of Marketing Research Consultants." *Industrial Marketing Management*, vol. 9 (February 1980), pp. 69–74.
> How to establish a good buyer-supplier relationship when contracting for outside market research consultants is the topic of this article.

M. M. Pressley. "Improving Mail Survey Responses from Industrial Organizations." *Industrial Marketing Management*, vol. 9 (July 1980), pp. 231–236.
> Pressley suggests specific techniques to improve response rate and timeliness.

E. M. Tauber. "How Market Research Discourages Major Innovation." *Business Horizons*, June 1974, pp. 22–26.
> Tauber warns that it is hard to do good market research on a very innovative product.

Part 3
THE PRODUCT

The third factor in managing profitable new product development is to have a product or technological idea that sets you apart from the competition. This is a solution idea. It answers the question of how you plan to capitalize upon the previously recognized problem idea. It is not enough to recognize an unfilled market need; you must also have a unique way to satisfy that need. I discuss how to come up with these ideas in Chapter 6 and how to evaluate them in Chapter 7.

6

Sources of Successful Ideas

KEY POINTS

Ideas can come from inside or outside the company.

A more useful categorization of idea sources is a need somewhere, a change somewhere, and previously abandoned ideas.

Companies can create a climate in which employees generate ideas.

Always be on the watch for licensing opportunities.

IDEA ORIGINATION

Although idea sources may be categorized as internal or external to the company, I categorize ideas as those arising from a need somewhere, those arising from a change somewhere, and those derived from old, previously abandoned ideas.

Ideas Based on a Need

Somebody in the company may observe that there is a need somewhere that has not yet been filled. It is well established that new product development efforts that try to exploit an un-

Try to fill real market needs.

filled need are more often successful than those that attempt to capitalize on the undirected output of the R & D department. Consequently, observations of the outside world are likely to lead to successful ideas. One would expect the marketing department to provide these external observations to the company, but top management, members of the board of directors, lawyers, bankers, and accountants are also coupled to the outside world. If you work with them, you are likely to recognize some unfilled needs.

Satisfied customers often have other needs you can fill.

Customers may also provide this kind of information. They may simply communicate a new need that has arisen with some member of the company. Sometimes a new unfilled need can be discovered by examining customer complaints or service records on previously delivered goods. In the latter case your company's service manager may very well turn out to be the source of useful new product development ideas.

Sometimes a supplier to the company will identify an unfilled need or alert you to competitor activity. The supplier may ask why you are not switching to new materials that your competitors have started to use.

Sometimes company management appears to be bereft of any new product development ideas and chooses to retain outside consultants to assist with this process. Such consulting help cannot guarantee to identify what will be a successful new product idea, but it may still be tremendously useful. For instance, the consultant may highlight that corporate goals as now formulated are inconsistent with market reality, thus identifying the need to reformulate corporate strategy.

Occasionally, there will be an unsolicited submission to the company from some external source. Such a source would ideally be a potential customer, but the unfilled need might be called to the attention of the company by the advertising agency or public relations firm or some similar group that is not itself a potential customer. Because an ownership claim may be made by the person who submits an unsolicited idea, every company must establish a legally safe way to handle these ideas.

Sometimes market needs can be validated by looking inside your company.

Unfilled needs within a company's own business very often provide a clue to an important new product development opportunity. For instance, DuPont, one of the world's largest chemical firms, recognized that it required certain analytic instruments within its own chemical laboratories. DuPont then custom built these instruments to satisfy their own needs. Subsequently, they offered these instruments for commercial sale to other companies. In this case the need for such instruments was validated by DuPont's own requirement for them and the general extrapolation from their needs to the recognition of a larger external market.

A company's R & D department or new product development department can also be the source of such ideas. Unfortunately, in the case of the R & D department, there is usually a tendency to look at technological possibility rather than market needs, which frequently results in a misdirected new product development effort. If, however, these R & D departments are looking at the outside world, they are as likely to come up with important opportunities as marketing, top management, or any other group. In general the characteristic of a winning idea is that it somehow saves purchasers money by permitting them to do something in a better way.

Be cautious about investing in technology without a clear market need.

Ideas that Capitalize upon Change

There are three kinds of change that provide opportunity to an alert company. The first of these may be called "eureka!" The second is legislation. The third is economic.

By "eureka" I mean the development of some new invention, a new process, or a new material. For instance, imagine that a new fiber material has suddenly been announced. If this material has a strength-weight ratio significantly higher than any other known material, then its use permits designers to make products differently. Consequently, certain structural elements might be made more compactly or in some other advantageous way. The cost, availability, and reliability of the new material will still be factors in its adoption.

Change is an opportunity for an alert company and a threat to others.

The enactment of legislation also provides a company with new opportunities. For instance, the passage of pollution control legislation has led to substantial new product opportunities for manufacturers of pollution control equipment. Unfortunately, there is a special risk whenever you set out to exploit new product development opportunities that have arisen because of legislation. You must be alert to the possibility that the legislation may be rescinded or subsequently modified, thus diminishing the apparent market opportunity.

Economic changes can also create opportunities. As an obvious and current example, the rapidly escalating price of energy has created opportunities for energy conserving products.

Old Ideas

Old ideas, previously abandoned, are frequently the source of very successful new product development opportunities. This phenomenon can occur whenever the reasons for the previous abandonment of the new product idea were due to conditions that have now changed significantly. For instance, perhaps a new material or component is now available, permitting the new product to be manufactured at a competitive low cost that was previously unattainable. Perhaps the market has changed; for instance, a key competitor has gone out of business. Perhaps the reason an old idea can now be successful is as simple as an expansion of your company's manufacturing capability. It may have grown to the size where it can efficiently produce the product now.

Review old ideas periodically.

To take advantage of old ideas, you must have carefully documented your reasons for abandoning the idea and the status of the design or development when you decided to do so. You must examine the file periodically, perhaps semiannually. Responsibility for this often is assigned to a corporate officer.

IMPROVING IDEA GENERATION

To enrich the flow of potentially winning ideas from internal sources, many companies have turned successfully to efforts to improve the creativity of the company staff. Broadly, creativity can be improved by making the company climate more receptive to creative efforts. In addition, adopting certain techniques, such as brainstorming, may specifically facilitate creativity.

Actively seek and encourage new ideas.

The climate for creativity within a company can be improved by having a receptivity rather than a hostility to new ideas. This implies a modest amount of freedom for people to work on new ideas. They also need some reasonable amount of support to bring these ideas to the point where they can be articulated. Encouragement, recognition, and appreciation for new ideas, even ones that are not adopted, must be the order of the day. Whenever ridicule or hostility is the reaction, one can be sure there will be fewer new ideas brought forth in the future. Texas Instruments has its IDEA (Identify, Develop, Expose, Action) program. There are about three dozen IDEA representatives scattered throughout the company. They can authorize funds for high-risk projects, many of which may fail.

Speak & Spell was initially supported and encouraged by an IDEA grant.

Brainstorming is often used to improve creativity; for instance, to identify some unfilled new product development opportunity. There are two broad approaches to brainstorming: the conventional (unaided) and the more productive approach in which a facilitator guides the process. Experiments have shown that the second approach produces more and better ideas. However, it requires an impartial facilitator. Thus, in some situations where a facilitator is not readily available it may be necessary to settle for the conventional process.

The conventional method for brainstorming is to advise perhaps a half-dozen people of the problem and convene a brainstorming meeting a day or two later. At this meeting restate the problem and reiterate the ground rules:

1. Absolutely no criticism (including smirking) permitted
2. The more ideas produced, the better
3. Novel, unusual (even impractical) ideas are desired
4. Improvement or combination of prior ideas is essential

Use a tape recorder to permit more leisurely subsequent consideration of the ideas thus generated. No judgment of the ideas is made during the brainstorming session itself.

To carry out the second, aided approach, a facilitator is chosen. The facilitator, typically an outsider such as a corporate staff person or a consultant, reviews the overall objective and guidelines that exist for the contemplated new product. Then participants in the brainstorming process are identified and the facilitator meets with each of them individually for about half an hour to elicit ideas. Next the facilitator sorts the ideas into appropriate categories and transfers them to posters (or a blackboard) in the meeting room. A few days later the brainstorming meeting is held in the usual way, except that the facilitator uses the posters for external stimulation. Recently, using this aided brainstorming process, one company was able quickly to identify several highly promising new product options based on unfilled market needs.

LICENSING

Licensing provides a way to take advantage of ideas others develop. There is a word of caution about this, however. Simply

Maintain a watch for licensing opportunities. because somebody else has developed an idea and is offering it for a license does not mean it is necessarily a good new product development opportunity. The fact that you are being offered the license may mean the inventor cannot exploit the idea successfully. However, in many cases a company will develop an idea outside its own business area. Then they may offer it for use under a license to other companies that are more suitably positioned to take advantage of it. In this later situation being alert for licensing opportunities may be a very good way to develop new products.

HIGHLIGHTS

An unfilled need that results in new product development may be brought to a company's attention by company personnel or management, customers, suppliers, outside consultants, or an unsolicited submission from someone outside the company.

A new technological development, new legislation, and economic changes may provide an alert company the chance to develop a new product.

Changing conditions may make a previously abandoned idea for new product development applicable.

Maintaining a climate of receptivity to innovation will encourage employees to generate ideas for new product development.

Brainstorming is a useful technique for improving creativity.

Licensing allows a company to take advantage of ideas developed by others.

FURTHER READING

R. E. Dutton. "Creative Use of Creative People." *Personnel Journal*, November 1972, pp. 818–822.
  Dutton gives detailed recommendations on how to provide an atmosphere conducive to creative individuals' being effective.

General Electric Company. *New Product/New Business Digest.*

Schenectady, New York: General Electric Company, annual.
> This describes hundreds of products and processes that are available for acquisition or licensing, abstracted from their monthly publication, Selected Business Ventures.

H. Geschka. "Introduction and Use of Idea-Generating Methods." *Research Management*, May 1978, pp. 25–28.
> This is a review of six idea generation techniques and the success achieved in their use.

H. Greenstein. "Licensing New Product Technology." *Industrial Research/Development*, June 1978, pp. 122–127.
> This is a thorough discussion of the issues involved in licensing.

W. Marcy. "Acquiring and Selling Technology—Licensing Do's and Don'ts." *Research Management*, May 1979, pp. 18–21.
> Here is specific, practical advice on what to do and avoid in licensing.

E. P. McGuire. *Generating New-Product Ideas.* Conference Board report 546. New York: Conference Board, 1972.
> This excellent booklet discusses creativity, internal and external sources of new product ideas, and licensing.

J. I. Peters. "Scavenging Successful New Products." *Industrial Research*, April 1973, pp. 52–55.
> This is a brief review of ways to identify new product opportunities, with stress on having a strategic framework and doing market research.

E. Raudsepp. "Play Games to Spark Your Creativity." *Chemical Engineering*, September 26, 1977, pp. 109–113.
> The author claims these exercise puzzles will stimulate creativity. They are fun, regardless of their actual utility.

E. Raudsepp and G. P. Hough, Jr. "Jumping to Solutions." *Psychology Today*, December 1977, pp. 75ff.
> Here are more exercise puzzles.

M. F. Rubenstein. "Problem Solving on Both Sides of the Brain." *Chemtech*, November 1981, pp. 654–657.
> The need to switch between convergent and divergent thinking to come up with good solutions to problems is the subject of this article.

M. Senkus. "Acquiring and Selling Technology—Licensing Sources and Resources." *Research Management*, May 1979, pp. 22–25.
> Here is a list of organizations to approach to seek licenses.

W. E. Souder and R. W. Ziegler. "A Review of Creativity and Problem Solving Techniques." *Research Management*, July 1977, pp. 34–42.

This is a discussion and listing of twenty techniques to help stimulate creativity and solve problems.

B. Twiss. "Creativity and Problem Solving." Chap. 3, pp. 66–90, in B. Twiss, *Managing Technological Innovation*, 2nd ed. London: Longman, 1980.

This is a thorough, general review of creativity and problem solving.

J. M. Utterback. "The Process of Innovation: A Study of the Origination and Development of Ideas for New Scientific Instruments." *IEEE Transactions on Engineering Management*, vol. EM-18, no. 4 (November 1971), pp. 124–131.

This report on a study indicates the need to integrate market information with technical information to generate successful ideas for new products. The author also stresses the value of outside consulting help.

E. A. von Hippel. "Has a Customer Already Developed Your Next Product?" *Sloan Management Review*, vol. 18, no. 2 (Winter 1977), pp. 63–74.

Von Hippel stresses the importance of working with innovative users and systematically trying to develop new products based on their needs.

7

Evaluation of Ideas

KEY POINTS

There are two crucial questions to keep in mind when undertaking new product development.

Checklists are useful, but do not rely on them because none is universally applicable.

There are fifty-four evaluation issues to consider whenever you think about a new product idea.

TWO CRUCIAL QUESTIONS

In undertaking a new product development effort, there are two crucial questions that must always be kept in mind: Can it be made? Can it be sold at a profit?

Companies often attempt to mechanize answering these two questions. Checklists, which are discussed extensively in the next section of this chapter, are often used to implement this mechanization. I discuss the issues involved in this chapter, but Part 4 contains the more extensive discussion of whether the product can be sold at a profit.

Can It Be Made?

The first key question concerns whether the product can be made. In answering it, there are basically three areas that must be considered: fundamental principles, product design, and product manufacture.

Fundamental Principles

Many ideas are rejected out of hand due to NIH—not invented here. There are in fact very few ideas that cannot work. Obviously, a perpetual motion machine violates the laws of thermodynamics and cannot work. Similarly, a product should not embody the requirement to transfer information or data faster than the speed of light, which is in fact a real limit on the design of computers today.

An idea may depend on a material having some properties that just are not reasonable. For instance, expecting a material to have properties that no known materials presently have is betting on an invention. That is okay if you want to take the risk. If you expect a threadlike diameter strut to have sufficient stiffness to support a very heavy weight on its top, somebody could calculate at what point Euler column failure would occur as well as the stiffness and other characteristics required. And if these properties were a couple of orders of magnitude beyond those of any known material, if the product depended on developing that material, I would argue you have small or no chance of success. Maybe at that point you want to turn to the R & D laboratory and say, "Look, we have this great product idea, but it depends on coming up with a material we do not think exists today. Would you do some checking for us? Would you do some development? If you could get into the ball park with something in the laboratory, then we will get serious about this new product. If you cannot, we are going to suspend work until the right material is developed."

The new product idea must be technically feasible.

Product Design

There are numerous questions in product design that determine whether the product can be made. The most important single issue is probably whether the design meets all market requirements. In thinking about this issue it is most important to consider not only the situation in the market today, but also in the future. This is especially important given the rapid pace of technological change. In addition, design criteria must be considered from the user's point of view, addressing such questions as functional suitability, lifetime, reliability, and service. The designers must even include a realistic appraisal of user

Anticipate the market need in the future, not just now.

skills. A product intended for secretaries will have an inherent market problem if it requires the secretary to know electronic engineering.

The next largest trap is probably the state of the specifications. Are these truly complete, and have the real requirements ("musts") been separated from the fringe benefits ("wants")? If not, the product will lack key features required for market access, or it will embody extra features and costs beyond market requirements.

After these two key issues with respect to design, there are a host of important issues such as transportation and storage conditions (for example, the product must typically survive a wide temperature range). Further, it is important to establish that patents do not preclude the design approach being taken. Finally, considering design criteria, the technical skills of the corporation, as well as the enthusiasm and drive of the people on whom the organization must depend to make the product, must be appropriate to the proposed product. For a low-technology shoe company to undertake a high-technology electronic new product development is to invite disaster.

Try to anticipate everything that can go wrong.

Product Manufacture

The third area to be faced is whether the product can be manufactured. A key ingredient here is the state of tolerances. If the product's fabrication depends on tolerances an order of magnitude tighter than those normally practiced, it is not likely you can successfully manufacture the product in the usual way. Another pitfall is dependence upon a single source of supply for a key component because that source may go out of business or suffer a major shutdown, such as a long strike.

The issue of realistic manufacturing cost targets is also crucial. The mere fact that the new product can be made and fully perform the desired functions is not satisfactory unless it can be made by available skills for appropriate costs. If the projected manufacturing cost is too high for the expected market application, it is just as fatal as if the product fails to perform a specified design function. Tooling, space, and other cost ingredients must also be considered in deciding whether the manufacturing cost target is realistic.

Get the manufacturing department to participate.

Can It Be Sold at a Profit?

At its simplest, this is merely a question of whether the price at which the product can be sold exceeds the cost at

Cost is set by internal factors and part costs; price is set by market factors.

which it can be developed. The issue is really deeper than this because there is significant uncertainty about both price and cost. Further, the bias on the part of product advocates is to underestimate development cost and overestimate selling price. Thus, a manager evaluating a proposed product is faced with a certain cost that must be borne but that has some uncertainty and is likely to increase, whereas he or she is expecting to achieve some rewards still further in the future. These expected rewards have an even greater uncertainty. This issue is complex and is discussed Part 4. In the following discussion I cover the key points.

Cost

In understanding cost there are three elements that must be considered: development expenses, continuing costs, and the lost profits of replaced products.

Development expenses include those that are fixed (for example, depreciation or laboratory equipment). These also are both certain and uncertain. *Continuing costs* are those associated with manufacturing the product when it is being produced and sold, including those associated with marketing, sales, and distribution. The likelihood of being financially successful at new product development is greatly increased by thorough and frequent estimation of all future costs. Financial analysis is relatively cheap compared to a failure.

If the proposed new product is a replacement for an existing product, you could have chosen not to undertake the new product development effort. You could merely continue to sell the existing product. Although the sales and attendant profit of the existing product might decline, this course of action would not require any unusual expense or cost on your part. Therefore, if a new product does make an existing product obsolete, one element of cost in new product development effort is the *lost profit of the replaced product*, which must be subtracted from projected profit of the new product.

Price

When there is no market, you can sometimes create one.

In thinking about price, there really are two subordinate questions: Is there a real market? What is the competition? The answers to these questions will establish the maximum price of the new product. To decide whether there is a real market, ask whether a need or want exists. If it does not, there must be a plan to create a need. Pet rocks and hula hoops satisfied created needs. But there are also many existing needs, the easiest to satisfy being a lower-priced substitute for a product that already is being purchased. After the existence of a need is established or the plan to create it is developed, it is necessary to ask whether customers really will buy the product. Do they have the money, and can the product be made available to them? Do they have any incentive to do so, or does it save them money?

The other issue that sets price is the existence of competition. If you are proposing to produce a product that could put another company out of business, that other company may react very aggressively to your entry into the marketplace. They probably are not just going to stand by and be put out of business. Conversely, if there is not much competition, it is much easier to maintain a high price.

The price you can charge is limited by need and competition.

It is always desirable to use a summary outline to focus critical thinking. The summary outline in Figure 7-1 follows the reasoning just presented. Each company has special situations and no single summary can address all the critical issues that fit these specialized situations, but Figure 7-1 is a useful skeleton that you can flesh out to suit your own needs.

Figure 7-1. Outline to focus critical thinking on new product development

I. Can it be made?
   A. Fundamental principles
      1. Does it violate the laws of physics?
      2. Does it require nonexistent properties of materials?
      3. Does it embody conflicting requirements?
   B. Design
      1. Are the specifications complete?
         a. Musts
         b. Wants
      2. Does it meet all market requirements?
         a. Now
         b. In future
         c. In use (lifetime, reliability, user skills, service)
      3. Can it be tested, verified, inspected?
      4. Can it be packaged, stored, distributed?
      5. Is it convenient to use and well styled?
      6. Does it violate any patents?
   C. Manufacture
      1. Are tolerances reasonable?
      2. Are there multiple sources of supply?
      3. Are people, tooling, and space available?
      4. Can cost targets be met?

II. Can it be sold at a profit?
   A. Cost
      1. Development
         a. Fixed and variable
         b. Certain and uncertain
      2. Continuing
         a. Manufacturing
         b. Marketing, sales, distribution, product improvement, and so forth
      3. Lost profits of replaced product(s)
   B. Price
      1. Is there a real market?
         a. Does a need or want exist?
            (1) Now or later
            (2) Alternative options
         b. Can the customer buy?
            (1) Availability of money
            (2) Constraints (legal, specifications, and so forth)
            (3) Distribution
         c. Will the customer actually buy?
            (1) Is the product functionally suitable?
            (2) What is customer's incentive?
            (3) Seasonality or cyclicality
            (4) Can our sales force sell it?
      2. What is the competition?
         a. Distinctive functional features
         b. Advertising, packaging, service
         c. Price levels
            (1) Now
            (2) Future trend
         d. Do barriers to entry of competition exist?
         e. Do preferred supplier relationships exist?

CHECKLISTS

Never rely solely on a checklist for new product evaluation.

Articles and books discussing marketing, research and development, and new product development frequently include checklists for the evaluation of new product ideas. In a sense the previous section of this chapter contained a checklist. Checklists may be useful if they are very carefully constructed for the specific business a company is engaged in. But you should not rely upon them exclusively or use them mechanically.

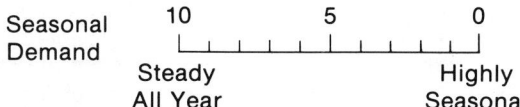

Figure 7-2. Checklist scale (for which labels are a construction problem) and ranking (for which respondent bias is a problem)

Checklist Problems

Published checklists usually start out with a listing of issues or factors to be considered and some kind of scale or ranking, as illustrated in Figure 7-2. Immediately, we can see two of the problems with a checklist. First, the construction of the scale must be specific to the company's business and cannot be generalized. For instance, a company that has a nonseasonal business would normally seek new products that also have steady demand all year. They would give that kind of product a high evaluation (for instance, a 10, as shown on the scale in Figure 7-2). Conversely, a company that already had a highly seasonal business (for example, a ski manufacturer) would be most interested in a counterseasonal product. Thus, they would value a highly seasonal product (reversing the scale) and would not be particularly interested in a product with steady, year-round demand.

No scale or ranking can be universally applicable.

The second problem illustrated in Figure 7-2 is the inevitable bias that creeps into the use of the checklist. All the check marks or ratings provided by the proponent of new product development will be for the two or three highest ranking fac-

The new product champion will always be biased.

TABLE 7-1 Distinctions Between Product Requirements in Different Companies

Type of Company	Industrial Product	Consumer Product	Aerospace Contractor	Service
Example of Typical Product	Laboratory Instrument, Power Supply	Candy, Clothing	Military Aircraft, Space Payload	Advertising, Cleaning
Profit Basis	Low Cost	Low Cost	High Cost	Low Cost
Number of Customers	Few/Many	Many	Few	Few/Many
Capital Requirement	Typically High	Usually High	Low	Low
Advertising Requirement	Sometimes	Yes	No	Yes
Packaging Requirement	No	Yes	No	No
Distribution System	Perhaps	Required	No	No

tors. They will never be for the poor or very poor ranking factors (or for the low numbers in a numerical scale).

The next issue that makes it difficult to use a generalized checklist is the fact that the kind of business in which the company is engaged significantly affects the importance of a given issue, as illustrated in Table 7-1. For example, packaging is often crucial for a consumer product company but unimportant for many other businesses.

A further problem with generalized checklists is that the significance of given issues changes with time. The following issues are important today but were not so twenty-five years ago:

1. Social and moral impact
2. Environmental impact
3. Recycling potential
4. Energy consumption
5. Safety

Today we might give very high significance to these other issues, which I generally like to lump under the title of "the front page of the *New York Times*." Approaching these issues from that point of view provides a way to deal with all social and environmental concerns. Ask yourself how you would feel if today's new product development actions were to appear on the front page of tomorrow's *New York Times*. If you feel that the product and the actions you are taking to develop it are ones you can be proud of, then you have probably met your social and environmental obligations. If not, perhaps you should rethink some aspect of the product.

Checklists, if used, must be revised periodically.

Checklists can never substitute for judgment and experience. The following list provides some of the technical problems that experience indicates can seriously delay or even scuttle a new product development effort. Rarely, however, can these kinds of problems be reduced to a simple checklist format.

1. Quality uniformity
2. New materials and components (sometimes)
3. Overengineering
4. Unreasonable tolerances
5. Too ambitious goals
6. Shortcuts
7. Contradictory specifications

Simple entries on a checklist, such as "Barriers to entry of competition," can be shorthand for a very large variety of possible factors. The following are some of the barriers that might exist:

1. Patent
2. License
3. Proprietary technology
4. Specification
5. Market domination

Having written a company specification for the product, even if it is widely accepted in the industry, is a far weaker barrier to entry of competition than a patent or truly proprietary technology. Thus, the proponent of the new product development idea might very well score it high on the barrier to entry of competition factor because there was a company-written specification with wide acceptance. However, that would in fact be a fairly weak barrier to entry of competition compared to alternative

The significance of a given factor depends on experience.

new product development ideas for which patents had been obtained.

The importance of a particular issue depends on the kind of product it is. For instance, for a routine order kind of product (such as office supplies) delivery reliability and price are typically the most important attributes as judged by the customer. Conversely, suppose your product is one for which the customer's personnel must be trained. Then technical service, ease of use, and the training you are prepared to offer would become the attributes judged most important by the customer.

What is critical for one product may not be critical for another.

An Approach to Checklist Construction

Despite the problems with checklists, they do have utility and it may very well be worth the effort for you to construct one for your own line of business. If you do so, I suggest you give each factor a two-value ranking, as illustrated in Figure 7-3. Thus, each factor or issue must be given both a value rank-

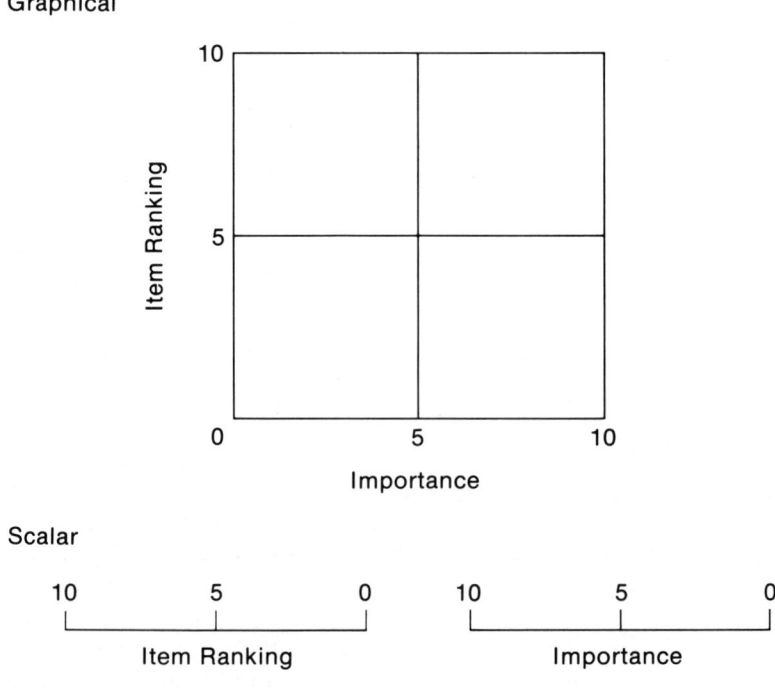

Figure 7-3. Bivalued checklist concepts

ing or score and an importance measure. After this is done, look at the factors of highest importance. Then look at those of lowest importance and ask yourself whether the high item rankings tend to correlate with the high importance issues or whether it is backward. I have not seen this approach used, but I believe it offers the potential for building useful checklists. An alternative is to use separate, perhaps scrambled, lists of item ranking and importance. However, always keep in mind that no purely mechanistic approach can ever be generally applicable. Judgment is still vitally important when trying to evaluate new product development ideas.

EVALUATION ISSUES

I have abstracted the following fifty-four evaluation issues from many published checklists.

- Advertising
- Ancillary support
- Application engineering
- Barriers
- Budget impact
- Champion
- Company skills
- Competition
- Consumer benefit
- Corporate attitude
- Delivery
- Distribution
- Engineering
- Financial factors
- Funding availability
- Industry outlook
- Internal considerations
- International considerations
- Inventory requirements
- Lead time

- Legal and regulatory requirements
- Manufacturing
- Market need
- Marketing
- Obsolete products
- Offshoots
- Patentability
- Pollution
- Potential for company
- Price and value consonance
- Production capacity
- Profit plan
- Promotion
- Proven or tested idea
- Quality image
- Raw materials
- Repairs
- Repeat purchase
- Research and development
- Safety
- Sales volume
- Seasonality
- Service
- Shelf life
- Social issues
- Spare parts
- Specifications
- Styling
- Technological threats
- Timing
- Unique benefits
- User environment
- Value added
- Warranty

Use this list whenever you consider a new product idea. It may be most fruitful to use it in qualitative form rather than in checklist form. (If you set out to construct a checklist for your own business, you might wish to use these evaluation issues as a starting point for factors to be evaluated.)

A checklist can sometimes be used qualitatively.

The list should stimulate thinking, not substitute for it. Each of the issues can become quite complex. For instance, Edwin Mansfield has observed, "R & D isn't worth anything alone. It has to be coupled to the market. The innovative firms are not necessarily the ones that produce the best technical output but the ones that know what is marketable" (*Business Week*, March 8, 1976). But a particular new product idea might very well be successful, even though there is no presently existing market, if the company had a good idea on how to develop a market or create demand. Sometimes such demand can be created to exploit new technology when the idea originated in the R & D laboratory rather than being created to fill existing market needs. In other cases new technology is not called for at all, merely appropriate stimulation of market need, as illustrated by hula hoops and pet rocks.

CASE HISTORIES

Plumbing Innovations

Imagine that your company is a plumbing supply company manufacturing faucets and other fixtures for use in residential buildings. Your manufacturing capability is built around machining brass and the subsequent application of chrome or other bright coatings to the machined brass. Your distribution is probably through hardware stores and plumbing supply outlets.

How would you use the previous list to evaluate the possibility of having an electronic faucet control? For instance, consider a new product embodying a touch-tone faucet control panel where you merely touched the temperature and volume settings you wanted. Regardless of your reaction to this idea, several of the enumerated evaluation issues suggest objectively the kind of consideration for which you should scrutinize the idea.

1. Company skills—there appears to be a mismatch with electronics required and machining presently available.

2. Distribution—The distributors are probably not familiar with electronics.
3. Internal considerations—The manufacturing division, heavily skilled in mechanical operations, is likely to feel threatened by the introduction of a product that does not use their present skills.
4. Market need—Is there any indication that consumers would indeed prefer or desire this kind of water control?
5. Manufacturing and production capacity—Present production capacity is clearly inappropriate for this product, and perhaps subcontractors would have to be the source of manufacturing.
6. Repairs and service—How are we going to provide service for this product, and how is the average plumber going to cope with a totally new product?
7. Safety—Can the voltage and current levels be kept low enough so that there is no hazard caused by a short circuit through the water?

I am not asking these questions to criticize this particular idea. Rather, they indicate how the evaluation issues can be used to flag significant questions. This can direct development effort to answer questions that are truly crucial to a particular new product development idea.

A Better Camera Lens

Most lenses for cameras are made up of several pieces of glass, all of whose surfaces are spherical. If one or more of the surfaces is made aspherical (nonspherical, but still a surface of revolution about an axis, which would be the optical axis of the lens system), then the completed camera lens could have fewer pieces of glass and higher optical quality, as illustrated in Figure 7-4. It is difficult routinely to manufacture aspherical lens surfaces in glass. It is easy to make aspheric surfaces in plastic, once a mold has been properly made, but plastic lenses are normally of inferior quality. However, a very thin plastic layer would not adversely affect lens quality. In 1974, one company conceived of the possibility of adding a very thin aspheric plastic layer to a spherical glass surface as a means to achieve the desired degree of asphericity.

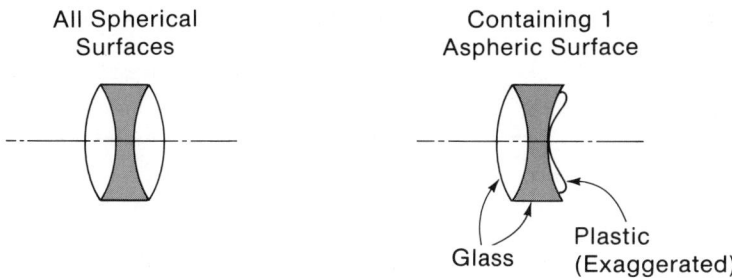

Figure 7-4. Aspheric by plastic layer addition to spherical substrate

The company that conceived this idea was a large distributor of camera lenses both in the United States and Europe. The company's lens manufacturing was done on contract by Japanese companies. In late 1974, the company's R & D manager learned that an English company was actually putting thin plastic layers on glass lenses in very limited quantities for a military application. It took all of 1975 to negotiate an agreement between the U.S. marketing and distribution company and the English lens manufacturing company. After more than a year of joint development work, the project was abandoned in 1977 because the Japanese lens manufacturers felt that their monopoly position would be threatened. They feared a manufacturing program in which one of the key pieces of glass for a lens had to be provided by an English company. In retrospect, this problem could have been foreseen much earlier. It would probably have been identified if people at the U.S. marketing and distribution company had thought through the evaluation issues, especially the need for an integrated manufacturing plan.

HIGHLIGHTS

- There are two key questions against which new product ideas must be evaluated: Can it be made? Can it be sold at a profit?
- Checklists may be helpful in answering these questions, but no generalized checklist that can be mechanically used will prove very helpful in the end.

The fifty-four evaluation issues listed in this chapter should be considered carefully when you deal with new product ideas.

FURTHER READING

D. R. Augood. "A New Approach to R & D Evaluation." *IEEE Transactions on Engineering Management*, vol. EM-22, no. 1 (February 1975), pp. 1–10.
> This is a highly mathematical, computer-based technique for evaluating new product ideas. The article is theoretical but has an extensive list of prior literature.

I. D. Canton. "How to Find Success in the Market." *Industrial Research/Development*, April 1979, pp. 103–108.
> Included here are a flow path diagram and a reasonable checklist.

D. S. Clifton, Jr., and D. E. Fyffe. "Comparative Rating of Product Ideas." In D. S. Clifton and D. E. Fyffe, *Project Feasibility Analysis*. New York: Wiley-Interscience, 1977.
> Table 2.1 is a useful thirty-four-item new product rating scale.

R. G. Cooper. "An Empirically Derived New Product Project Selection Model." *IEEE Transactions on Engineering Management*, vol. EM-28, no. 3 (August 1981), pp. 54–61.
> Cooper presents a thorough, somewhat academic new product selection method. He cites thirteen factors. He claims great success by validation on numerous real cases, but fails to give any instructions on how to apply the technique.

E. B. Frech. "Scorecard for New Products: How to Pick a Winner." *Management Review*, February 1977, pp. 4–11.
> This is a nineteen-item new product scorecard used by an industrial product company.

J. T. Gerlach and C. A. Wainwright, "Guidelines for Successful New Products." Chap. 9, pp. 127–131, in J. T. Gerlach and C. A. Wainwright, *Successful Management of New Products*. New York: Hastings House, 1968.
> This is a narrative listing of eight items to consider for consumer products.

G. W. Jones. "New Product Development." *Conference Board Record*, September 1976, pp. 25–28.

Here are ten points to consider for retail store consumer products.

W. B. Locander and R. W. Scamell. "Screening New Products—A Two Phase Approach." *Research Management*, March 1976, pp. 14–18.
This is a list of twenty criteria for new products.

C. J. Mathey. "New Approaches to the Management of Product Planning." *Research Management*, November 1976, pp. 13–18.
This article contains a detailed screening form.

E. P. McGuire. *Evaluating New-Product Proposals*. Conference Board report 604. New York: Conference Board, 1973.
This excellent booklet thoroughly reviews practices for both industrial and consumer products.

J. W. Muncaster. "Picking New Product Opportunities." *Research Management*, July 1981, pp. 26–29.
Muncaster lists twenty-nine items to rate for industrial products.

A. Paolini, Jr., and M. A. Glaser. "Project Selection Methods that Pick Winners." *Research Management*, May 1977, pp. 26–29.
The authors present a mathematical method to use for financial screening very early in the new product development effort.

B. M. Richman. "A Rating Scale for Product Innovation." Chap. 23, pp. 319–333, in R. R. Rothberg, ed., *Corporate Strategy and Product Innovation*. New York: Free Press, 1976.
This brief review of how to allocate resources to new product opportunities contains an eight-factor evaluation matrix.

B. Twiss. "Project Selection and Evaluation." Chap. 4, pp. 91–120, in B. Twiss, *Managing Technological Innovation*, 2nd ed. London: Longman, 1980.
This general review of issues includes a forty-seven-item list of evaluation criteria.

D. L. Vrable. "Social and Environmental Considerations in New Product Development." *Journal of Marketing*, vol. 36 (October 1972), pp. 11–15.
This is a review of nontraditional issues to consider in the evaluation of new product ideas.

G. R. White and M.B.W. Graham. "How to Spot a Technological Winner." *Harvard Business Review*, March–April 1978, pp. 146–152.
White and Graham present a general framework to evaluate new product opportunities that arise from technological development.

Part 4

THE PROFIT PLAN

The fourth critical factor is a plan to make money. You can have a brilliant strategy, recognize an unfilled market need, devise a prize-winning product to satisfy that need, and still lose money. In this part I review how to decide if you can make enough money to justify the effort (Chapter 8). I also review how to deal with the uncertainty of predicting what will occur with your new product development effort (Chapter 9).

8

Financial Analysis

KEY POINTS

You must be able to demonstrate that a new product development program will be profitable.

The Profit MAP is a straightforward way of analyzing profit potential.

Internal rate of return can be used to analyze prospective investments.

Five estimated quantities determine the internal rate of return.

Each financial measure has its own sensitivity to changes in the five estimated quantities.

PROGRAM FINANCIAL JUSTIFICATION

Consider the case of the computerized axial tomographic (CAT) scanner, developed by an English company, EMI. EMI's technical director, Godfrey Hounsfield, received the joint Nobel prize for medicine for developing the CAT scanner. "Rarely can a Nobel prize for scientific achievement have been followed so closely by a booby prize for business failure as in the case of the CAT scanner business of Britain's EMI" (*Business Week*, May 19, 1980, p. 40). "Although the scanner was one of the outstanding advances in medical sciences in recent decades, EMI was unable to make it a financial success" (*The Wall Street Journal*, April 30, 1980).

It is vital to assure yourself that a new product development program you will propose has a prospective financial return commensurate with the inherent risk it entails. Just as you would try to sell a product to a Frenchman by speaking French, new product development programs must be justified to financially oriented top management. Consequently, it is necessary to translate program justifications into financial terms. Winning the Nobel prize, despite the attendent prestige, just is not good enough.

Suppose you can get $6 for selling a product that costs you only $5 to produce and sell. That is a pretax profit of $1 per $6 of sales, or about 8 percent after-tax profit on sales. That profit rate exceeds the earning rate of the vast majority of American companies. Would you like to propose such a new product development program to your management? As you will see shortly, profit rate is only one financial issue you must consider.

Although different companies use different financial justification techniques, most now use the internal rate of return (IRR) to evaluate major investments. Thus, if new product development programs can be described in terms of IRR, these programs and their approvals are put on the same footing as capital investment approvals, for instance, whether to build a new warehouse. When presented this way, new product development programs frequently will show very attractive returns. But if these programs do not show attractive returns, perhaps they should not be funded.

Financial analysis helps you allocate limited resources.

The *Profit MAP* is designed to calculate IRR, as well as other common financial measures. The Profit MAP (MAP is an acronym for Measurements to Assess Programs) provides a straightforward format for quickly analyzing a new product development program's profit potential. Assuming basic data are available, use of the Profit MAP requires only a pencil and several minutes of work. Using the Profit MAP will help you identify any critical areas requiring more detailed examination. Because it summarizes the involvement of all departments, you can use the Profit MAP to aid communication with the other functional managers involved in the program.

IRR can be calculated quickly.

The Profit MAP is structured to be primarily useful for those programs aimed at new product introduction. Exploratory R & D, aimed at discovery of new phenomena, for instance, is best scrutinized in other ways. Similarly, many routine marketing programs can be evaluated against other criteria, although the Profit MAP will frequently be helpful for daily decisions, such as pricing. The Profit MAP can also be used to evaluate new facility projects, capital asset procurements, manufacturing capacity expansion, and similar investments, allowing you to consider all investment opportunities on a comparable basis.

If you do not know what method of financial analysis your company now uses, make inquiries and find out. This is crucial for two reasons. First, you want to be sure any new product program you advocate is well justified by your company's own standards. Second, you want to know enough either to do the analysis yourself or to be able to check the reasonableness of someone else's calculations.

INTERNAL RATE OF RETURN

IRR is one of several financial measures corporations use to analyze the attractiveness of prospective investments. Profit margin, payback period, return on investment, and present value are some other financial measures, but each of these has substantial drawbacks. *Profit margin* is simple but does not contain any information about the investment required to obtain the profit margin, nor does it provide any measure of risk. Although *payback period* (Figure 8-1) ignores everything that occurs after payback, it is a simple and useful indicator of risk because a long payback period is more risky than a short payback period. Return on investment (ROI) is certainly an important calculation (Figure 8-2). However, for future investments it can be done only on a period-by-period basis (for example, fiscal year) or it must be averaged over some longer time period. ROI is also a generic label for any of several measures (Figure 8-3); so it can be ambiguous. You should understand precisely which return measure(s) your own company uses. In common with the two preceding measures, ROI fails to account for the time value of money. Net present value (NPV), which does reflect the time value of money, is related to IRR, but NPV requires that a discount rate be preselected. Both NPV and IRR are forms of discounted cash flows (DCFs), in which money in future years is taken to have less value than today's money. Each of these techniques, and many others, is treated in financial texts in more detail.

IRR depends on the timing of expenses and receipts, thus recognizing the time value of money. Fortuitously, calculation

IRR is normally preferred for financial analysis of new product programs.

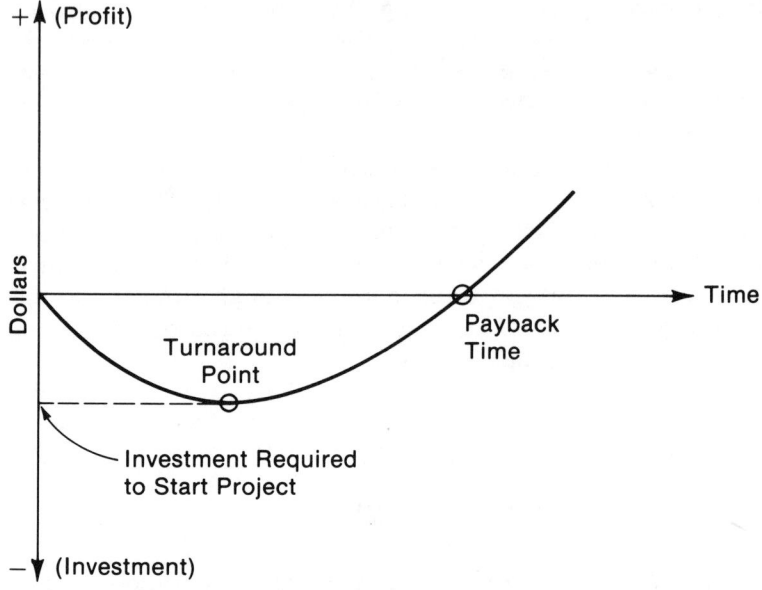

Figure 8-1. Payback period

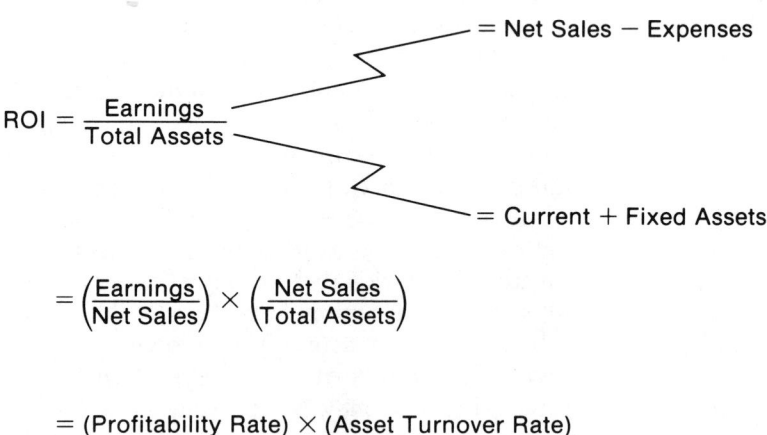

Figure 8-2. Return on investment

of IRR with the Profit MAP provides all the information to permit quick determination of the other measures. The inherent assumption in IRR is that recovered funding is reinvested into

- Return on Investment

$$\text{ROI} = \frac{\text{Net Income (After Tax)}}{\text{Shareholders' Equity} + \text{Debt}}$$

- Return on Equity

$$\text{ROE} = \frac{\text{N.I.}}{\text{S.E.}}$$

- Return on Total Capital

$$\text{ROTC} = \frac{\text{N.I.} + \text{After-Tax Interest on Debt}}{\text{S.E.} + \text{Debt}}$$

- Return on Assets

$$\text{ROA} = \frac{\text{N.I.}}{\text{Total Assets (Depreciated) on Balance Sheet}}$$

- Return on Assets Employed

$$\text{ROAE} = \frac{\text{N.I.}}{\text{Total Assets} + \text{Accumulated Depreciation} + \text{Value of Leased Facilities}}$$

Figure 8-3. Other measures of financial return

the same venture, at the venture's rate of return. IRR is the rate by which the cash flow must be discounted, such that the total discounted cash flow is equal to zero over the period representing the life of the investment, for instance, ten years. Expressed another way, IRR is the discount rate for which the program's NPV is zero. Thus, IRR provides a direct comparison against the cost of money and is the prevailing method employed in many financially sophisticated companies.

USING THE PROFIT MAP

My illustration of the use of the Profit MAP to assist with the solution of typical new product development problems will provide you with a simple tool for daily use.

Required Data

To calculate IRR, you must know the total cash flow for each year of the program (or venture or project or development). To determine cash flow, you must make five assumptions or estimates for each year:

1. Company sales resulting from the development program
2. Manufacturing costs attendant to the sales
3. Development expense to achieve the sales
4. Operating costs attendant to the sales and
5. Capital expenditures to permit production, distribution, and so forth

If you cannot calculate a program's IRR, you do not know enough about it.

It may seem like a lot of work to obtain this information, but it simplifies justification. It is prudent to make these estimates before engaging in a program rather than persisting in an unprofitable program. If you lack the information to make these five estimates, that is a clear danger signal that your program's ultimate success depends on unknowns. Therefore, the work required to make the estimates is an essential ingredient of a successful program. Because each of the five quantities is an estimate, the derived IRR is an estimate. Nevertheless, it takes only an hour or so to analyze a proposed development program's IRR and its sensitivity to the assumptions. In doing this analysis, you will gain a great deal of insight.

Five estimated quantities determine the IRR.

The top portion of the Profit MAP shows a tabular form in which these five estimated quantities can easily be listed. Everything else on the Profit MAP depends solely on what you enter in the top five lines. The numbers entered by hand on lines 1 to 5 of Figure 8-4 are an example of the kind of estimates (in thousands or millions of dollars) that might be made. Company sales (line 1) should be estimated by the marketing department or be derived from market research, and the estimate must reflect market reality. Criteria by which sales estimates may be made include the value of the proposed new product substitution to the customer, the sales volume of similar products, market share estimates where market size is known, or the number of units to be sold multiplied by price per unit. Use market research, as discussed in Part 2, to improve these estimates whenever possible. It is important that sales volume be consistent with manufacturing and distributing capacity.

Use market research to improve estimates.

The manufacturing and technical development people should estimate manufacturing cost (line 2). They can use the cost of similar products, a component parts list cost multiplied by a suitable markup factor, or, ideally, a detailed product breakdown and manufacturing plan. When the manufacturing rate will be nonuniform, it may also be helpful to use an order-mix simulation.

Development expenses (line 3) may occur in marketing, manufacturing, certainly will occur in R & D, and perhaps will occur in other departments; so each concerned department must provide appropriate estimates, ideally from detailed plans, including contingency.

Operating costs (line 4) are usually related to sales and might typically be some percentage of sales, say 25 percent or 30 percent. Each concerned department should provide these estimates from detailed plans.

Each department concerned in the development must estimate capital expenditures (line 5). These should include transportation and installation costs when applicable, as well as contingency. The estimates and the assumptions upon which they are based are crucial in determining the calculated quantities. The next chapter discusses how this sensitivity can be elucidated.

Determining Total Cash Flow

The other eight quantities (lines 6 through 13) in the top part of the Profit MAP are merely arithmetic manipulations of the five estimated quantities for each year of the analysis, typically ten years. [Bracketed] numbers on the Profit MAP are negative, in accordance with conventional financial notation. The Profit MAP has been set up so that once the five estimated quantities are entered, it is very easy to calculate the resulting cash flow. The specific calculations required are listed under "derivation." Lines 7, 8, 10, and 11 are merely addition or subtraction of quantities in lines above. The following sections discuss lines 6, 9, 12, and 13.

Depreciation

Depreciation (line 6) can be taken in accordance with company practice or as in the Profit MAP as 10 percent per year (that is, straight-line depreciation for a ten-year life). Figure 8-5 illustrates a few common depreciation schedules. In general, companies prefer short (and accelerated) depreciation schedules because these will improve the IRR.

Assume that a $1,000 investment is made on the first day of the fiscal year, that the asset has a five-year useful life with no salvage value, and that the investment tax credit, if any, is ignored.

Depreciation Schedule \ Year	1	2	3	4	5
Straight-Line (20% per Year)	200	200	200	200	200
Declining Balance (40% of Balance)	400	240	144	86	52
Sum-of-the-Years-Digits, Remaining Life $\frac{5}{15}, \frac{4}{10}, \frac{3}{6}, \frac{2}{3}, \frac{1}{1}$	333	267	200	133	67

Figure 8-5. Various depreciation options

Income Tax

Income tax (line 9) can be calculated at the company income tax rate or as in the Profit MAP, assumed to be 50 percent of the before-tax income.

Working Capital Increase

The working capital increase (line 12) is the funding it takes to support a growing business to finance inventory and accounts receivable. Company practice may provide a guide for what this should be, although it is probably 25 percent to 35 percent of the sales increase of the current year compared to the previous year. The Profit MAP is constructed on the assumption of 30 percent (Figure 8-6). Although the amount on line 12 can be calculated exactly for any given situation, the Profit MAP provides a simple way to insert a reasonable estimate of the cash required. As a general rule, (1) rapid sales increases, (2) low profits, and (3) long periods between incurring costs and getting paid all increase the working capital required. The reverse lowers it.

To get a better feeling for the notion of the *working capital increase* (as it is commonly called), think of it as the cash required to pay your bills prior to being paid by your customers.

PROFIT MAP

CASH FLOW

QUANTITY	DERIVATION	YEAR (N) 1	2	3	4
1 COMPANY SALES	ESTIMATE			1	3
2 MANUFACTURING COST	ESTIMATE				
3 DEVELOPMENT EXPENSE	ESTIMATE				
4 OPERATING EXPENSE	ESTIMATE				
5 CAPITAL EXPENDITURES	ESTIMATE				
6 DEPRECIATION	$(0.1) \times \sum_{1}^{N} 5$				
7 GROSS PROFIT	1-2				
8 BEFORE TAX INCOME	7-3-4-6				
9 INCOME TAX	$(0.5) \times 8$				
10 NET INCOME	8-9				
11 OPERATING CASH FLOW	6 + 10				
→ 12 WORKING CAPITAL INCREASES	$(0.3) \times (1_N - 1_{N-1})$				0.6
13 TOTAL CASH FLOW	11-5-12				

Figure 8-6. Working capital increase example

Consider the case in which you get paid $6 for something that costs you $5 to make and sell, which provides a nice profit. Assume you must pay the $5 of cost (for example, materials purchased from suppliers and wages for your workers) three months before you are repaid $6 by your customer. Assume your sales, and therefore your costs, increase 10 percent per month. This profitable growth situation (Figure 8-7) continues to require a cash investment as long as the sales continue to increase, even when money begins to flow in from customers. You use this cash investment, the so-called working capital increase, to finance your inventory (raw material, work in process, and finished goods) and accounts receivables. You can easily see that the cash position at the end of the fourth month and later would be worse if the customer paid later, if profits were less, or if the rate of sales increase was more rapid. When sales flatten out and decline, the venture begins to generate cash.

A product can be profitable, but you can run out of cash.

Total Cash Flow

The *total cash flow* (line 13) is the predicted amount of actual cash required (if line 13 is negative) or generated (if line 13 is positive) each year. This is not the same as *after-tax income,* as illustrated in Figure 8-8. Total cash flow differs from after-tax income because of *capital expenditures* (a cash outlay that cannot be expensed in determining taxable income), *depreciation* (the noncash "expense" allowed as a tax deduction for

110 The Profit Plan

Month Sale	1	2	3	4	5	6	7	8	9
First	<5>			6					
Second		<5.5>			6.6				
Third			<6.05>			7.26			
Fourth				<6.66>			7.99		
Fifth					<7.32>			8.78	
Sixth						<8.05>			9.66
Etc.									
Net Cash for Month	<5>	<5.5>	<6.05>	<0.66>	<0.72>	<0.79>			

Figure 8-7. The reason for working capital increases

	After-Tax Income	Cash Flow	
		No Capital Investment	With Capital Investment
Sales	1,000	1,000	1,000
Manufacturing Cost	− 500	− 500	− 500
Gross Margin	500	500	500
Operating Expense	− 300	− 300	− 300
Depreciation	− 50		
Before-Tax Income	150		
Income Tax	− 75	− 75	− 75
After-Tax Income	75		
Capital Investment			− 500
	75	125	− 375

Difference Is Depreciation — Difference Is Capital Investment

Figure 8-8. Cash flow and after-tax income

prior capital expenditures), and *working capital* (the money it takes to finance or run the venture).

In the last year of the financial analysis (whatever year it may be), it is conventional to assume that the venture is *liquidated*, which means that the total cash flow for that year is the sum of what is calculated normally plus the summation of all the working capital increases to date. This is just another way of saying that the assets on the balance sheet are being sold off in the final year. This adjustment is noted at the end of line 13 of the Profit MAP.

Calculating the IRR

IRR may be calculated now in two ways from the total cash flow. First, many business pocket calculators have an IRR function, and you may use this. If you have to make many IRR calculations, it is best to use a pocket calculator or a business computer. Alternatively, you can calculate the discounted cash flows (DCF) simply by using discount factors as multipliers for each of the entries in the total cash flow line. The *discount factors* are present value amounts for the various discount percentages. Thus, the discount factor is $(1 + R)^{-(N-1)}$ where R is the discount percentage expressed fractionally and N is the year. These discount factors are printed on the lower portion of the Profit MAP. In Figure 8-4, this calculation has been done for two discount percentages (20 percent and 25 percent). When each of these DCFs is calculated, the cumulative DCF (that is, the NPV at that discount percentage) can then be calculated. The cumulative DCF that is equal to zero provides the discount percentage that is the value of IRR. The grid at the bottom left corner of the Profit MAP may be used to interpolate and thus estimate the IRR value at which the NPV is zero. To bracket the zero-crossing quickly, calculate the NPV at 25 percent discount. If it is negative, calculate the NPV at 10 percent discount. If the 25 percent NPV is positive, calculate the NPV at 40 percent discount.

There are two ways to calculate the IRR from the total cash flow.

Having the total cash flow, you can easily determine the payback period by looking at the cumulative cash flow and determining in which year it turns, and remains, positive. Line 14 is included on the Profit MAP for this purpose.

There is one caution to observe in this method of program financial analysis. If the program goal is to produce a replacement product, you must subtract the profits the existing product would have produced had it not been replaced in the appropriate years.

Significance of IRR

What is the significance of an IRR value, say the 24.6 percent in the base case example (Figure 8-4)? At the simplest, the IRR value of alternative investments can be compared, and resources can then be committed to the most promising undertaking(s).

The IRR allows comparison of alternative investments.

For example, assume you can obtain a 12 percent yield (before tax) on funds invested in some security issued by the United States government, which is the safest investment you can find. This is equivalent to a 6 percent after-tax return, a value that can be compared to the IRR (which is also an after-tax value). In this case, we can say that there is a 100 percent certainty that a U.S. security investment will return 6 percent after taxes. As long as we have 25 percent confidence that the alternative (Figure 8-4) investment will go according to plan, we would favor it (only slightly, however, because 0.25 × 24.6 percent is 6.1 percent, which is only a trifle better than the 6.0 percent return for the U.S. security). To put it another way, the risk factor in a venture must discount the IRR to allow comparison of investment opportunities.

Your company's basic strategy, and the reasons you have for undertaking new product development, as discussed in Part 1, should establish your minimum IRR target. As a general rule, forecasted new product development IRR values should exceed 20 percent, or perhaps 30 percent, because of the risk. If the forecasted IRR value is lower, there probably is a better investment available elsewhere.

There is a general caution about IRR or any other financial analysis. Such analyses involve assumptions such as the estimates on lines 1–5, the applicable tax rate, and the required working capital. Consequently, the actual return from the investment may differ from the calculated return. Thus, sometimes you should still undertake a new product development program or make a capital investment when the calculated IRR is low. This may be the lesser of evils in some situations. For instance, developing a new attachment to your existing product might have a marginal financial return, but this development could prevent a competitor from gaining access to your customer base.

There frequently are intangible factors not amenable to analysis. Consider a decision whether to make a capital investment in a new word processor system. You can estimate the value of the labor saved precisely, but it is harder to assess the value of being able to produce typing more quickly, if you can quantify it at all. And the value of being able to produce perfectly typed documents with justified margins is intangible.

Therefore, you should use IRR as a guide rather than an absolute criteria. If a thoroughly analyzed new product program has a high IRR (for instance, greater than 20 percent), it is probably a good undertaking, even though it should still be judged against other investment opportunities. If the calculated IRR is low (for instance, less than 10 percent), look around for a better new product investment opportunity, or, if you go ahead, understand the financial risk you are taking. In between these extremes, you must recheck assumptions and not just change the numbers because you do not like the calculated IRR. In these intermediate cases, you may find it helpful to use the probabilistic techniques that I describe in the next chapter, and you will have to rely to some extent on judgment. Do not, however, go ahead with a program that has a low IRR just because someone in R & D or marketing says new product development is inherently risky. With careful screening and thoughtful analysis, you can improve your success rate. Finally, if you do not have enough information to estimate the IRR, that is a danger signal warning you that you do not yet know enough about the proposed development program.

IRR must not be the only factor in a new product development decision.

Sample Calculation

The numbers in Figure 8-4 show the completed sample calculation. Numbers in brackets are negative. Line 13 is the resulting cash flow. The cumulative cash flow (line 14) indicates that the payback occurs in the seventh year.

The bottom portion of the Profit MAP contains the discount factors for seven discount percentages, and two lines have been filled in. The rate at which the DCF is equal to zero is approximately 24.5 percent, as graphically derived, and this is therefore the IRR. The following step-by-step procedure is used:

1. Make ten-year estimates of sales, manufacturing cost, development expense, operating cost, and capital investment and enter these on lines 1, 2, 3, 4, and 5, respectively.

2. Calculate the next eight lines for each of the ten years. In Figure 8-4, the following are the calculations for year 5:

   Line 6: $0.1 \times 1 = 0.1$
   Line 7: $2.88 - 1.15 = 1.73$
   Line 8: $1.73 - 0 - 0.58 - 0.1 = 1.05$
   Line 9: $0.5 \times 1.05 = 0.53$
   Line 10: $1.05 - 0.53 = 0.52$
   Line 11: $0.1 + 0.52 = 0.62$
   Line 12: $0.3 \times (2.88 - 2.4) = 0.14$
   Line 13: $0.62 - 0 - 0.14 = 0.48$

3. Multiply each of the total cash flow amounts (line 13) by the discount factors for the 25 percent discount percentage (in year 5, this is 0.41), and add each of these ten discounted amounts to obtain the NPV for that discount percentage.

4. If this NPV is positive, repeat this multiplication and summation for the 40 percent discount percentage (and, for better accuracy, the 35 and 30 percent lines) to permit estimation of IRR. If the NPV is negative, repeat the multiplication and summation for the 10 percent discount rate (and, for better accuracy, the 15 and 20 percent lines) to permit estimation of IRR. (In the text and Figure 8-4, I have used only the 25 percent and 20 percent discount percentages, graphically estimating IRR as 24.5 percent. Exact calculation yields 24.63 percent.)

5. To obtain the cumulative cash flow (line 14), from which the payback period is determined, sum up all the cash flows to the current year. In the example, for year 5 (1.20) + (0.2) + (0.15) + 0.41 + 0.48 = (0.66).

COMPARISON OF FINANCIAL MEASURES

Each financial measure has a different sensitivity to any change in the five estimated quantities. To illustrate this, consider four alternatives for the investments being made during the first two years of the base case (Figure 8-9). Although payback period, NPV, and IRR all yield the same relative ranking (that is, case D is most attractive and case B is least attractive), return on investment is not sensitive in the same way. This anomaly arises because return on investment is not depen-

	Case = Base		A		B		C		D	
QUANTITY	1	2	1	2	1	2	1	2	1	2
1 COMPANY SALES										
2 MANUFACTURING COST										
3 DEVELOPMENT EXPENSE	0.5	0.5	0.5	0.5	1.0	1.0	0.5	0.5	0.25	0.25
4 OPERATING EXPENSE										
5 CAPITAL EXPENDITURES	1.0		2.0		1.0		0.5		1.0	

	Base	A	B	C	D
•Years 1 & 2					
Total "Start-Up" Charges	2	3	3	1.5	1.5
•Year 5					
Gross Margin % (7 ÷ 1)	60	60	60	60	60
Profit Rate % (10 ÷ 1)	18	16.5	18	19	18
ROI % (10 ÷ Σ5)	52	24	52	110	52
•Entire Program					
NPV at Discount Factor = 20%	0.36	(0.38)	(0.09)	0.58	0.74
Maximum Negative Cumulative Cash Flow (in Year 3)	(1.55)	(2.4)	(2.05)	(1.3)	(1.13)
Payback Period (Approximate Years)	6.1	7.1	6.9	5.6	5.5
IRR%	24.6	16.7	19.2	28.2	31.9

Figure 8-9. Comparison of several financial measurements (All cases have same sales, manufacturing cost, and operating cost in years 3 through 10.)

dent on noncapital expenditures, namely, the initial development expense (line 3). Return on investment is thus undesirable for evaluating new product development programs. The discretionary investment you, as a manager, must make involves both expensed and capitalized items, and you want to be able to measure the return on the combination.

In common with all financial measures except NPV, IRR does not reflect the absolute size of the investment. For instance, a program with an IRR of 25 percent that has sales of $100 million might be better than an alternative with an IRR of 30 percent if the latter had sales in the same time period of only $10 million. Thus, although IRR is an excellent way to assess your new product development program, you should still use judgment and not rely entirely on myopic numerical analysis.

Financial measures all have different sensitivities to changes in the five estimated quantities.

TABLE 8-1 IRR Sensitivity to Estimates

Case	IRR %
Base Case	24.6
−10% Development Expense	25.3
−10% Capital	25.8
−10% Operating Expense	25.8
−10% Manufacturing Cost	27.0
+10% Sales	29.7

IRR SENSITIVITY TO ESTIMATE ASSUMPTIONS

As noted, the five estimated quantities completely determine the resultant financial measures. Therefore, it is important to ascertain the sensitivity of IRR (or any other financial measure, such as NPV) to the assumptions. You can do so quickly by altering each assumed quantity and calculating a new IRR. For instance, each estimated quantity can be improved by 10 percent of the assumed value for all years being estimated and the resultant IRR calculated (Table 8-1). In this instance, the sales and manufacturing cost estimates are most critical. Thus, in a real situation you might choose to examine these in more detail. In general, IRR will always be most sensitive to sales. However, the relative ranking of the other four estimated quantities (lines 2 through 5 of the Profit MAP) will vary, depending on the specific numbers.

IRR AS AN R & D/MARKETING MANAGEMENT TOOL

Consider the following hypothetical situation. You are the manager of a new product development program (Figure 8-10). At the end of the first year of the program a revolting development becomes apparent: design complexity causes manufacturing costs 25 percent higher than the original plan, namely, 50 percent of sales rather than 40 percent. The following three alternatives are proposed (Figure 8-11):

PROFIT MAP — Alternative X

CASH FLOW

QUANTITY	YEAR (N) DERIVATION	1	2	3	4	5	6	7	8	9
1 COMPANY SALES	ESTIMATE		2	6	10	15	15	12	9	5
2 MANUFACTURING COST	ESTIMATE		1	3	5	7.5	7.5	6	4.5	2.5
3 DEVELOPMENT EXPENSE	ESTIMATE	1	0.6	0.2						
4 OPERATING EXPENSE	ESTIMATE		0.6	1.8	3	4.5	4.5	3.6	2.7	1.5
5 CAPITAL EXPENDITURES	ESTIMATE									

PROFIT MAP — Alternative Y

CASH FLOW

QUANTITY	YEAR (N) DERIVATION	1	2	3	4	5	6	7	8	9
1 COMPANY SALES	ESTIMATE			2	6	10	15	15	12	9
2 MANUFACTURING COST	ESTIMATE			0.8	2.4	4	6	6	4.8	3.6
3 DEVELOPMENT EXPENSE	ESTIMATE	1	1	0.6	0.2					
4 OPERATING EXPENSE	ESTIMATE			0.6	1.8	3	4.5	4.5	3.6	2.7
5 CAPITAL EXPENDITURES	ESTIMATE									

PROFIT MAP — Alternative Z

CASH FLOW

QUANTITY	YEAR (N) DERIVATION	1	2	3	4	5	6	7	8	9
1 COMPANY SALES	ESTIMATE		2	6	10	15	15	12	9	5
2 MANUFACTURING COST	ESTIMATE		0.8	2.4	4	6	6	4.8	3.6	2
3 DEVELOPMENT EXPENSE	ESTIMATE	2.2	0.6	0.2						
4 OPERATING EXPENSE	ESTIMATE		0.6	1.8	3	4.5	4.5	3.6	2.7	1.5
5 CAPITAL EXPENDITURES	ESTIMATE									

Figure 8-11. Alternative consequences after revolting development

1. (X) Continue on the current schedule but settle for manufacturing costs that are 50 percent of the sales price rather than the previously estimated 40 percent.
2. (Y) Spend an extra year and $1.0 million in development to reduce the manufacturing cost to the original plan, but accept a one-year delay.
3. (Z) Spend an extra $1.2 million in R & D development expense in the next year to recover the original plan.

Figure 8-11 shows only the estimate numbers that are changed with respect to Figure 8-10 to clarify which assumptions have been changed. The calculations now commence in year 1 with

CASH FLOW   X: IRR = 29.6 %

QUANTITY	YEAR (N) / DERIVATION	1	2	3	4	5	6	7	8	9	10
1 COMPANY SALES	ESTIMATE		2	6	10	15	15	12	9	5	
2 MANUFACTURING COST	ESTIMATE		1	3	5	7.5	7.5	6	4.5	2.5	
3 DEVELOPMENT EXPENSE	ESTIMATE	1	0.6	0.2							
4 OPERATING EXPENSE	ESTIMATE		0.6	1.8	3	4.5	4.5	3.6	2.7	1.5	
5 CAPITAL EXPENDITURES	ESTIMATE										
6 DEPRECIATION	$(0.1) \times \sum_1^N 5$										
7 GROSS PROFIT	1-2		1.0	3	5	7.5	7.5	6	4.5	2.5	
8 BEFORE TAX INCOME	7-3-4-6	(1.0)	(0.2)	1	2	3	3	2.4	1.8	1	
9 INCOME TAX	$(0.5) \times 8$	(0.5)	(0.1)	0.5	1	1.5	1.5	1.2	0.9	0.5	
10 NET INCOME	8-9	(0.5)	(0.1)	0.5	1	1.5	1.5	1.2	0.9	0.5	
11 OPERATING CASH FLOW	6 + 10	(0.5)	(0.1)	0.5	1	1.5	1.5	1.2	0.9	0.5	
12 WORKING CAPITAL INCREASES	$(0.3) \times (1_N - 1_{N-1})$		0.6	1.2	1.2	1.5	0	(0.9)	(0.9)	(1.2)	
13 TOTAL CASH FLOW	11-5-12	(0.5)	(0.7)	(0.7)	(0.2)	-0-	1.5	2.1	1.8	3.2	

CASH FLOW   Y: IRR = 35.8 %

QUANTITY	YEAR (N) / DERIVATION	1	2	3	4	5	6	7	8	9	10
1 COMPANY SALES	ESTIMATE			2	6	10	15	15	12	9	
2 MANUFACTURING COST	ESTIMATE			0.8	2.4	4	6	6	4.8	3.6	
3 DEVELOPMENT EXPENSE	ESTIMATE	1	1	0.6	0.2						
4 OPERATING EXPENSE	ESTIMATE			0.6	1.8	3	4.5	4.5	3.6	2.7	
5 CAPITAL EXPENDITURES	ESTIMATE										
6 DEPRECIATION	$(0.1) \times \sum_1^N 5$										
7 GROSS PROFIT	1-2			1.2	3.6	6	9	9	7.2	5.4	
8 BEFORE TAX INCOME	7-3-4-6	(1)	(1)	-0-	1.6	3	4.5	4.5	3.6	2.7	
9 INCOME TAX	$(0.5) \times 8$	(0.5)	(0.5)	-0-	0.8	1.5	2.25	2.25	1.8	1.35	
10 NET INCOME	8-9	(0.5)	(0.5)	-0-	0.8	1.5	2.25	2.25	1.8	1.35	
11 OPERATING CASH FLOW	6 + 10	(0.5)	(0.5)	-0-	0.8	1.5	2.25	2.25	1.8	1.35	
12 WORKING CAPITAL INCREASES	$(0.3) \times (1_N - 1_{N-1})$			0.6	1.2	1.2	1.5	-0-	(0.9)	(0.9)	
13 TOTAL CASH FLOW	11-5-12	(0.5)	(0.5)	(0.6)	(0.4)	0.3	0.75	2.25	2.7	4.95	

CASH FLOW   Z: IRR = 36.7 %

QUANTITY	YEAR (N) / DERIVATION	1	2	3	4	5	6	7	8	9	10
1 COMPANY SALES	ESTIMATE		2	6	10	15	15	12	9	5	
2 MANUFACTURING COST	ESTIMATE		0.8	2.4	4	6	6	4.8	3.6	2	
3 DEVELOPMENT EXPENSE	ESTIMATE	2.2	0.6	0.2							
4 OPERATING EXPENSE	ESTIMATE		0.6	1.8	3	4.5	4.5	3.6	2.7	1.5	
5 CAPITAL EXPENDITURES	ESTIMATE										
6 DEPRECIATION	$(0.1) \times \sum_1^N 5$										
7 GROSS PROFIT	1-2		1.2	3.6	6	9	9	7.2	5.4	3	
8 BEFORE TAX INCOME	7-3-4-6	(2.2)	-0-	1.6	3	4.5	4.5	3.6	2.7	1.5	
9 INCOME TAX	$(0.5) \times 8$	(1.1)	-0-	0.8	1.5	2.25	2.25	1.8	1.35	0.75	
10 NET INCOME	8-9	(1.1)	-0-	0.8	1.5	2.25	2.25	1.8	1.35	0.75	
11 OPERATING CASH FLOW	6 + 10	(1.1)	-0-	0.8	1.5	2.25	2.25	1.8	1.35	0.75	
12 WORKING CAPITAL INCREASES	$(0.3) \times (1_N - 1_{N-1})$		0.6	1.2	1.2	1.5	-0-	(0.9)	(0.9)	(1.2)	
13 TOTAL CASH FLOW	11-5-12	(1.1)	(0.6)	(0.4)	0.3	0.75	2.25	2.7	2.25	3.45	

Figure 8-12. Cash flows and IRR for the three alternatives of Figure 8-11

the amounts that were originally (Figure 8-10) in year 2 because IRRs are always calculated for future investments and cash flows and thus ignore prior events. These data (Figure 8-11) reflect the three alternatives facing your development team. Completion of these calculations (Figure 8-12) reveals the following IRR percentages: alternative X = 29.6 percent; alternative Y = 35.8 percent; and alternative Z = 36.7 percent. Thus, these simple calculations reveal that the additional development expense of alternative Z, although it is substantial and must be borne immediately, is your most attractive alternative. The calculations also spotlight other issues: Is the extra money to fund alternative Z really available? Are people and space to implement this alternative also available? In the case of alternative Y, is a one-year delay in reaching the market truly acceptable? These factors may outweigh the higher IRRs, which could lead to the choice of alternative X or further exploration to identify another alternative.

The Profit MAP is used for future cash flows. That is, the first year starts when the analysis is being done, which is not necessarily the start of the program. Prior expenses are like water over the dam. The total of the working capital increases are added into the total cash flow in the last year, which in these three alternatives is year 9.

IRR calculations always start at the present time.

This same kind of analysis can be done to evaluate other managerial choices, such as the trade-off between adding people (for example, more salespersons) or acquiring equipment (for example, radiotelephones for existing salespersons' cars).

PRICING DECISIONS

Pricing is a common problem that may confront you as the manager of new product development. In those situations where price versus volume trade-offs are known (or can be determined by test marketing), the Profit MAP provides a convenient format to determine an optimal price point (Figure 8-13).

EFFECT OF PREMATURE CANCELLATION

Very often corporate management will want to understand what happens if the proposed development effort must be ter-

Assume base case sales are units at $5.00 each (that is, 400,000 units in year 3). Is it better to sell 300,000 units at $6.00 each?

Approach:

PROFIT MAP

CASH FLOW

QUANTITY	YEAR (N) DERIVATION	1	2	3	4	9	10
1 COMPANY SALES	ESTIMATE			1.8			
2 MANUFACTURING COST	ESTIMATE			0.6			
3 DEVELOPMENT EXPENSE	ESTIMATE	0.5	0.5				
4 OPERATING EXPENSE	ESTIMATE				0.3		
5 CAPITAL EXPENDITURES	ESTIMATE	1.0					

$1.8 = \$6.00 \times 300{,}000$

$0.6 = 0.8 \times \dfrac{300{,}000}{400{,}000}$

$0.3 = 0.4 \times \dfrac{300{,}000}{400{,}000}$

To be filled in with same growth, leveling, and decline pattern as base case.

⟶ IRR = 28%, Which is better than base case (24.6%)

Figure 8-13. Use of Profit MAP to assist with price versus volume trade-off decision

minated early. This is commonly determined by truncating the venture in the ninth or eighth or other year and calculating the IRRs for these shorter efforts (Figures 8-14 and 8-15). This is another way to judge the risk of a contemplated venture.

HIGHLIGHTS

- Internal rate of return is frequently used to evaluate major investments.
- The Profit MAP can be used to calculate IRR and other common financial measures.
- To determine cash flow, which you must do to calculate IRR, you must determine five estimated quantities: company sales resulting from the program, attendant manufacturing costs, development expense, operating costs, and capital expenditures.

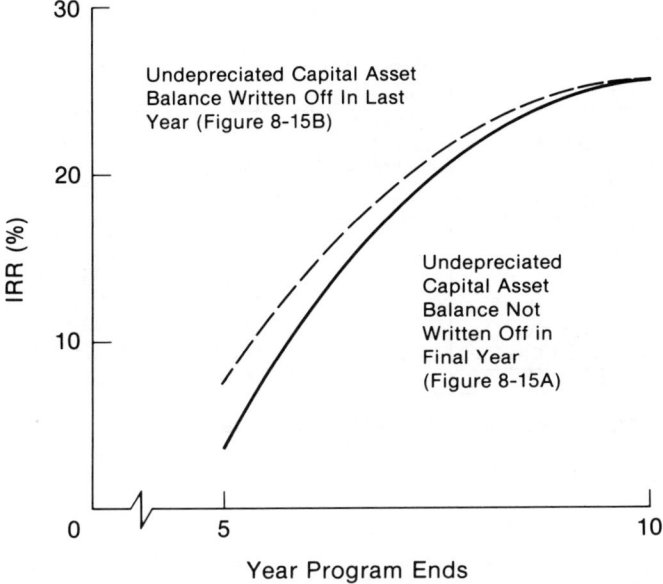

Figure 8-14. Effect of premature cancellation of base case example

Financial measures each have a different sensitivity to any change in the five estimated quantities.

IRR is a measure usually most sensitive to sales.

The Profit MAP can be used to help with pricing decisions.

FURTHER READING

R. J. Brown. "A New Marketing Tool: Life-Cycle Costing." Chap. 36, pp. 465–471, in R. R. Rothberg, ed., *Corporate Strategy and Product Innovation*, 2nd ed. New York: Free Press, 1981.
  Brown discusses the buyer's financial analysis issues.

B. T. Gale and B. Branch. "Cash Flow Analysis: More Important Than Ever." *Harvard Business Review*, July–August 1981, pp. 131–136.
  This is a good summary of the importance of cash flow and its relation to return on investment.

PROFIT MAP

CASH FLOW

QUANTITY	DERIVATION	YEAR (N) 1	2	3	4	5
1 COMPANY SALES	ESTIMATE			2.0	2.4	2.88
2 MANUFACTURING COST	ESTIMATE			0.8	0.96	1.15
3 DEVELOPMENT EXPENSE	ESTIMATE	0.5	0.5			
4 OPERATING EXPENSE	ESTIMATE			0.4	0.48	0.58
5 CAPITAL EXPENDITURES	ESTIMATE	1.0				
6 DEPRECIATION	$(0.1) \times \sum_1^N 5$	0.1	0.1	0.1	0.1	0.1
7 GROSS PROFIT	1-2			1.2	1.44	1.73
8 BEFORE TAX INCOME	7-3-4-6	(0.6)	(0.6)	0.7	0.86	1.05
9 INCOME TAX	$(0.5) \times 8$	(0.3)	(0.3)	0.35	0.43	0.53
10 NET INCOME	8-9	(0.3)	(0.3)	0.35	0.43	0.52
11 OPERATING CASH FLOW	6 + 10	(0.2)	(0.2)	0.45	0.53	0.62
12 WORKING CAPITAL INCREASES	$(0.3) \times (1_N - 1_{N-1})$	-0-	-0-	0.6	0.12	0.14
13 TOTAL CASH FLOW	11-5-12	(1.2)	(0.2)	(0.15)	0.41	1.34

A - Remaining depreciation not taken in last year

PROFIT MAP

CASH FLOW

QUANTITY	DERIVATION	YEAR (N) 1	2	3	4	5
1 COMPANY SALES	ESTIMATE			2.0	2.4	2.88
2 MANUFACTURING COST	ESTIMATE			0.8	0.96	1.15
3 DEVELOPMENT EXPENSE	ESTIMATE	0.5	0.5			
4 OPERATING EXPENSE	ESTIMATE			0.4	0.48	0.58
5 CAPITAL EXPENDITURES	ESTIMATE	1.0				
6 DEPRECIATION	$(0.1) \times \sum_1^N 5$	0.1	0.1	0.1	0.1	0.6
7 GROSS PROFIT	1-2			1.2	1.44	1.73
8 BEFORE TAX INCOME	7-3-4-6	(0.6)	(0.6)	0.7	0.86	0.55
9 INCOME TAX	$(0.5) \times 8$	(0.3)	(0.3)	0.35	0.43	0.28
10 NET INCOME	8-9	(0.3)	(0.3)	0.35	0.43	0.27
11 OPERATING CASH FLOW	6 + 10	(0.2)	(0.2)	0.45	0.53	0.87
12 WORKING CAPITAL INCREASES	$(0.3) \times (1_N - 1_{N-1})$	-0-	-0-	0.6	0.12	0.14
13 TOTAL CASH FLOW	11-5-12	(1.2)	(0.2)	(0.15)	0.41	1.59

B - Asset balance written off in last year

Figure 8-15. Cash flows for base case example, assuming program ends in year 5

S. R. Goodman. "Using Return on Investment for New Product Development." Chap. 27, pp. 360–371, in R. R. Rothberg, ed., *Corporate Strategy and Product Innovation.* New York: Free Press, 1976.

Goodman discusses discounted cash flows to evaluate new product development efforts.

R. H. Hayes and W. J. Abernathy. "Managing Our Way to Economic Decline." *Harvard Business Review,* July–August 1980, pp. 67–77; and R. H. Hayes and D. A. Garvin. "Managing as if

Tomorrow Mattered." *Harvard Business Review*, May–June 1982, pp. 70–79.

> These two articles point out the hazards of relying solely on financial analyses when making investment decisions.

G. F. Mechlin and D. Berg. "Evaluating Research—ROI is not Enough." *Harvard Business Review*, September–October 1980, pp. 93–99.

> This is a discussion of the need to consider nonfinancial issues when evaluating basic research programs.

Profit MAP. Rosenau Consulting Company, Santa Monica, Calif., 1980.

> This is a single-page, color-coded blank form with brief instructions to permit manual calculation of IRR or NPV.

H. T. Spiro. "Capital Budgeting." Chap. 8 in H. T. Spiro, *Finance for the Non-Financial Manager*. New York: Wiley-Interscience, 1978.

> This is a basic discussion of various financial measures.

H. A. Tombari. "To Buy or Not to Buy?" *Production Engineering*, March 1978, pp. 50–53.

> Tombari provides simple examples of payback period, return on investment, NPV, and IRR.

B. Twiss. "Financial Evaluation of Research and Development Projects." Chap. 5, pp. 121–147, in B. Twiss, *Managing Technological Innovation*, 2nd ed. London: Longman, 1980.

> Most of this chapter is academic, but there is a discussion of DCF.

Uncertainty and Probability

KEY POINTS The financial outcome of any new product development program is uncertain.

An IRR ogive can be used to portray the uncertainty.

The Gaussian method and the Monte Carlo method can be used to calculate IRR distributions.

IRR PROBABILITY DISTRIBUTIONS

Uncertainty

New product development programs have an uncertain outcome.

The previous chapter showed how you can easily calculate internal rate of return and apply it to the management of your new product development programs. However, all such programs are typically fraught with uncertainty about how the future may actually turn out. Therefore, it is also useful to be able to reflect this kind of uncertainty in using IRR. The same is true if return on investment, payback period, or some other financial measure is used. Rather than say a program has an IRR of, for instance, 26.9 percent, it is more realistic to say that the program has a range of anticipated IRR values, and the planned IRR is 26.9 percent. A simple way to communicate this uncertainty is to talk about an expected likelihood that a particular value of IRR will be obtained, that is, an expected distribution of the IRR values. This chapter demonstrates simple techniques for calculating expected probability distributions of IRR.

As a way to introduce this concept, consider the following hypothetical situation. Suppose two outcomes seem equally certain:

1. Your proposed development program will succeed as per plan (for instance, as illustrated in Figure 8-4) and sales volume, manufacturing and operating costs, and development and capital expenses will be as per plan.
2. Your development program will take an extra year of development time with attendant development expenses and only 80 percent of the planned sales will be achieved.

In both situations you assume that manufacturing cost will be 40 percent of sales, operating cost will be 20 percent of sales, and capital investment is $1.0 (thousands or millions) in the first year.

The planned situation (Figure 8-4) has a projected IRR of 24.6 percent, whereas the hypothetical, equally likely situation has a projected IRR of 14.9 percent. Although the mathematically expected value of IRR is the average of these two projections, namely, 19.75 percent, it is more descriptive to say it is certain that the IRR will be greater than 14.9 percent and 50 percent certain that it will be as great as 24.6 percent. We can also say it is certain that the projected IRR will not be more than 24.6 percent. This, of course, is a very simple example. It indicates that it is equally likely that the IRR will be 14.9 percent or 24.6 percent.

Probabilistic IRR Distributions

Usually, there is a continuous distribution of expected IRR values (Figure 9-1). The bell-shaped curve indicates that an IRR of 25 percent is most likely to occur and that there is virtually no likelihood of an IRR of less than 10 percent or greater than 40 percent. This particular case is a normally distributed

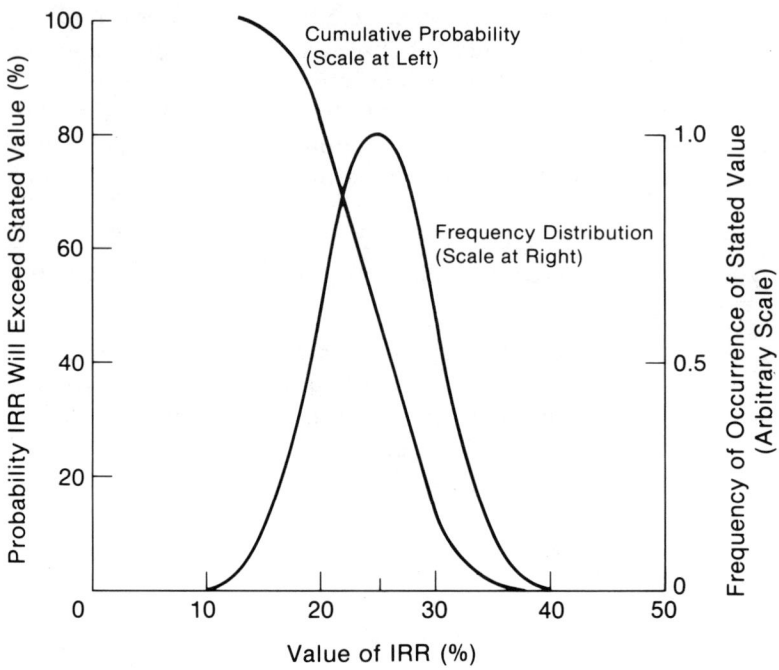

Figure 9-1. Distributions of IRR values

The uncertainty can be portrayed by an IRR ogive.

(Gaussian) frequency distribution with a mean of 25 percent and a standard deviation [σ] of 5 percent. The sloping curve is a cumulative frequency distribution, or *ogive*, of the same data. It indicates that there is a 100 percent probability that the IRR will exceed 10 percent and virtually no likelihood that it will exceed 40 percent. In this case, because the frequency distribution is symmetrical about the IRR value of 25 percent, the ogive has a probability value of 50 percent at an IRR value of 25 percent. Although either a frequency distribution curve or an ogive can be used to describe the expected range of IRR values, I will use ogives for this purpose.

Consider two hypothetical distributions (Figure 9-2). These ogives both show that it is 50 percent likely that an IRR of 25 percent will be achieved. In case II, there is a larger spread of expected IRR values; so it is more likely that lower values will be obtained. But in case II, higher IRR values than case I could be obtained. A company accustomed to taking risks might be more likely to engage in program II than program I because

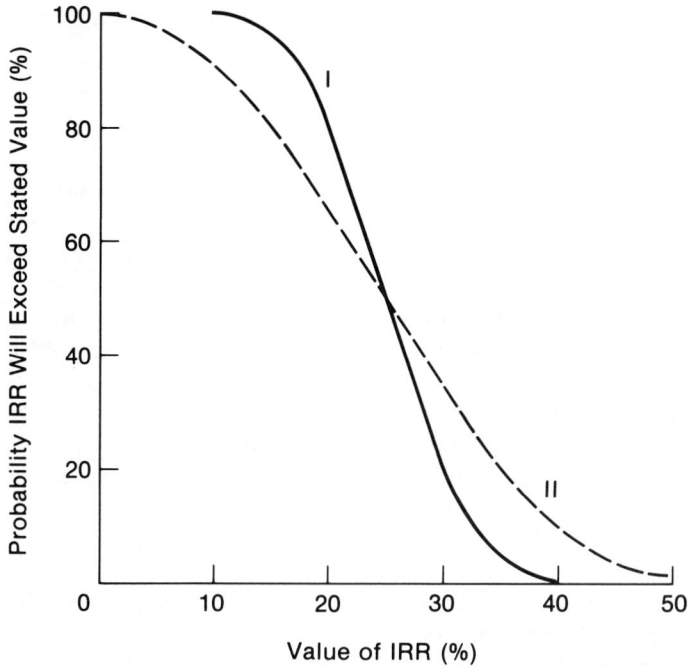

Figure 9-2. Two cases with different risk characteristics

program II has a greater likelihood of achieving high IRR values. Frequently, alternatives being evaluated will also have ogives with 50 percent values that are different for each alternative, as well as having different spreads of expected IRR values.

CALCULATING IRR OGIVES

Bascially, there are two easy methods for calculating IRR distributions; the *Gaussian method* and the *Monte Carlo method*. In the Gaussian method, all five estimated quantities (see Chapter 8) are assumed to be normally and symmetrically distributed about the mean value (that is, the plan or base case) and independent of each other. In the Monte Carlo method, each of the five estimated quantities is independently estimated as to the likelihood of occurrence without any restriction as to the distribution or symmetry of values.

Gaussian Method

In the Gaussian method, the assumption is made that the base (or plan or reference) case is approximately correct. But instead of being fixed, each of the five estimated quantities is uncertain, thus raising or lowering the IRR estimate. To illustrate this first calculation method, assume that the situation in Figure 8-4 constitutes the plan, which thus becomes the base case.

The assumption is made that small changes in each of the five estimated quantities will result in a change in IRR that is linear over the range of change. This assumption saves a great deal of time and underlies the technique used in this first method of calculating the IRR ogive. The perturbations of the five estimated quantities are assumed to be uniform multiples (for example, 0.85, 1.1, and so on) of the quantity over the entire ten-year life of the venture. This linearity assumption is nearly correct (Figure 9-3), which illustrates the IRR values

The Gaussian method is quick but limited.

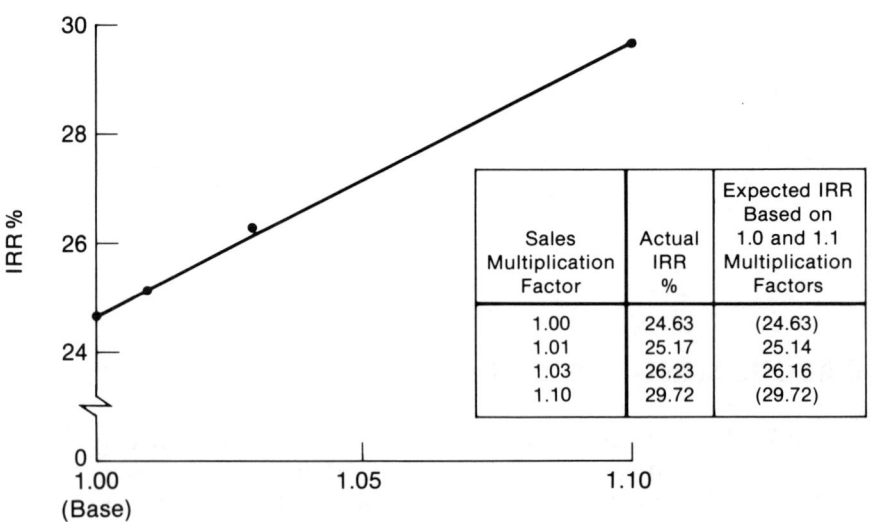

Figure 9-3. Linearity of IRR change with sales multiplication factor change

that result from making multiplicative changes in only the estimated sales of the base case.

No general statement can be made that this linearity assumption will always be valid. However, it is reasonable, at least for small perturbations, and it is a useful simplifying approximation. This simplification is also reasonable considering that this entire method deals with quantities that are future estimates, which are inherently uncertain. So if you need only an approximate ogive, any small ogive errors attributable to the linearity assumption may be not too important.

The following case illustrates this first method. Given sensitivity coefficients for the previous base case (Figure 8-4) as shown in Table 9-1 and distributions in the estimated quantities (Table 9-2) you can calculate the resulting distribution of IRR (Figure 9-4). This calculation assumes each quantity's variability is independent of the others. The ogive is most easily drawn with the aid of arithmetic probability graph paper, although a table of the normal (Gaussian) probability function may also be used.

Monte Carlo Method

The second, more general method to calculate IRR ogives is actually to enumerate the five estimated quantities for the al-

TABLE 9-1. Sensitivity Coefficients for Determining IRR Change Due to Perturbation of the Base Case Assumptions for Each of the Five Estimated Quantities

Situation	IRR%	Absolute Change in IRR per 1% Change in Estimated Quantity
Base Case	24.6	—
Development Expense Reduced 10%	25.3	−0.07
Capital Expense Reduced 10%	25.8	−0.12
Operating Costs Reduced 10%	25.8	−0.12
Manufacturing Costs Reduced 10%	27.0	−0.24
Sales Increased 10%	29.7	+0.51

TABLE 9-2. Assumed Standard Deviations of Estimated Quantities, Expressed as a Percentage Variation about Base Case Values

Estimated Quantity	Standard Deviation of Multiplier Factor About 1.0
Sales	10%
Manufacturing Costs	3%
Development Expense	20%
Operating Costs	1%
Capital Expense	5%

Sales $\quad\sigma_S = 10\%,\ \Sigma_S = 0.51\ \sigma_S$
Manufacturing Costs $\quad\sigma_M = 3\%,\ \Sigma_M = 0.24\ \sigma_M$
Development Expense $\quad\sigma_D = 20\%,\ \Sigma_D = 0.07\ \sigma_D$
Operating Costs $\quad\sigma_O = 1\%,\ \Sigma_O = 0.12\ \sigma_O$
Capital Expense $\quad\sigma_C = 5\%,\ \Sigma_C = 0.12\ \sigma_C$

$$\sigma_{IRR} = \{(\Sigma_S)^2 + (\Sigma_M)^2 + (\Sigma_D)^2 + (\Sigma_O)^2 + (\Sigma_C)^2\}^{1/2} = 5.4\%$$

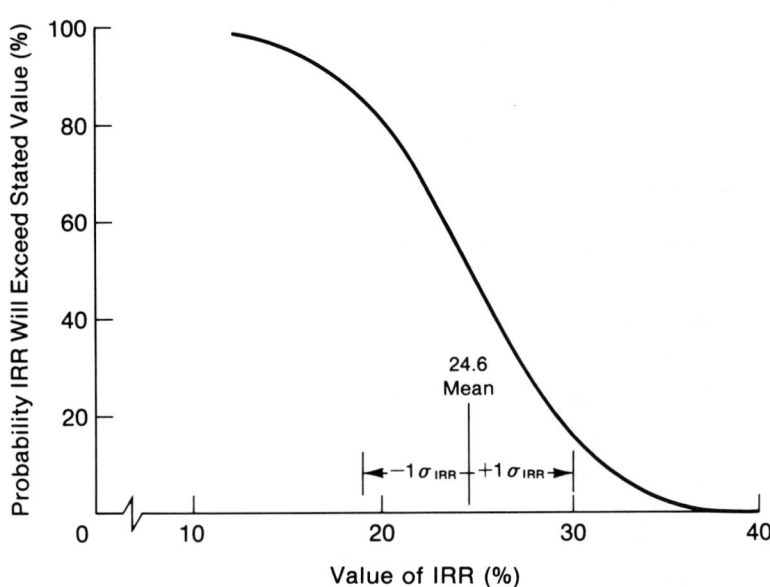

Figure 9-4. Gaussian Ogive

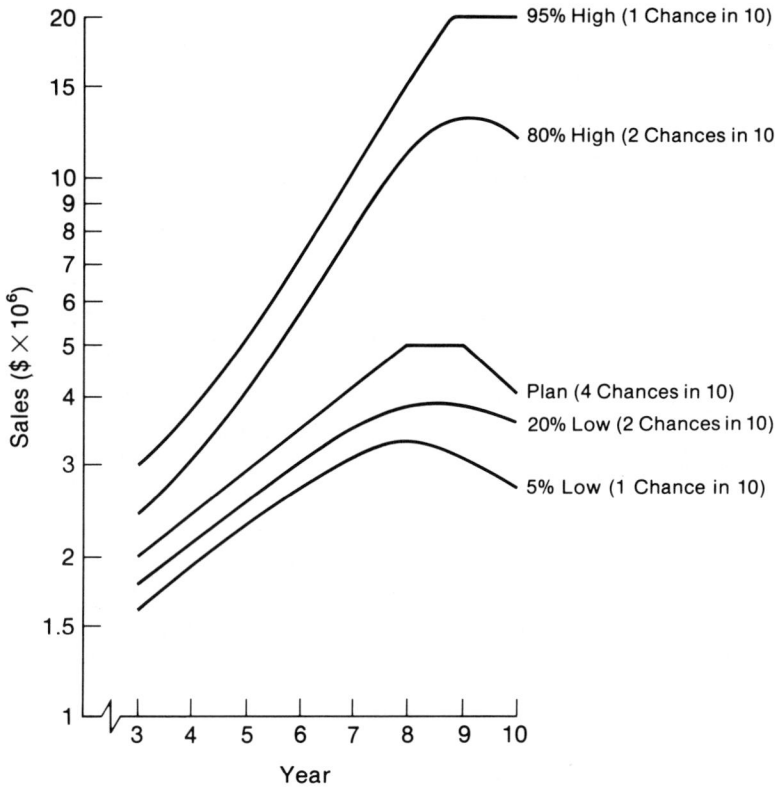

Figure 9-5. A probabilistic sales forecast

ternative scenarios, including their expected frequency of occurrence. Then many values of IRR are calculated, each IRR value depending on a random selection of various scenarios for the five estimated quantities. For instance, suppose the expected sales are forecast with a range of likelihoods (Figure 9-5). This might reasonably be the kind of estimate that the marketing department or a market research consultant could provide, using methods such as those discussed in Part 2. Notice in this illustration that the "95% high" sales scenario is asymmetrically higher than the "plan" by an amount more than the "5% low" scenario is lower than plan. This kind of asymmetrical assumption is possible with the Monte Carlo method but not with the Gaussian method. This particular sales estimate and comparable data for the other four estimated quantities constitute the required input data (Table 9-3).

The Monte Carlo method is flexible.

TABLE 9-3. IRR Probability Input Generation Worksheet (Ranges of random numbers can be changed)

Quantity	Estimate	Random Number	Value of Quantity in Year (N)									
			1	2	3	4	5	6	7	8	9	10
1	95% high	01-10			3	4	5	7	10	15	20	20
	80% high	11-30			2.4	3	4	6	8	11	13	12
Company	Plan	31-70			2	2.4	2.88	3.46	4.15	4.98	4.98	4.15
Sales	20% low	71-90			1.8	2.2	2.7	3.1	3.7	3.9	3.8	3.6
	5% low	91-00			1.6	2.0	2.4	2.8	3.3	3.3	3.1	2.8
2	5% low	01-10	35%									
	20% low	11-30	38%									
Manufacturing	Plan	31-70	40%	}	Of Company Sales							
Cost	80% high	71-90	44%									
	95% high	91-00	50%									
3	5% low	01-10	0.25	0.25								
	20% low	11-30	0.4	0.4								
Development	Plan	31-70	0.5	0.5								
Expense	80% high	71-90	0.7	0.7								
	95% high	91-00	1.0	1.0								
4	5% low	01-10	17%									
	20% low	11-30	19%									
Operating	Plan	31-70	20%	}	Of Company Sales							
Cost	80% high	71-90	22%									
	95% high	91-00	25%									
5	5% low	01-10	0.8									
	20% low	11-30	0.9									
Capital	Plan	31-70	1.0									
Expenditures	80% high	71-90	1.2									
	95% high	91-00	1.5									

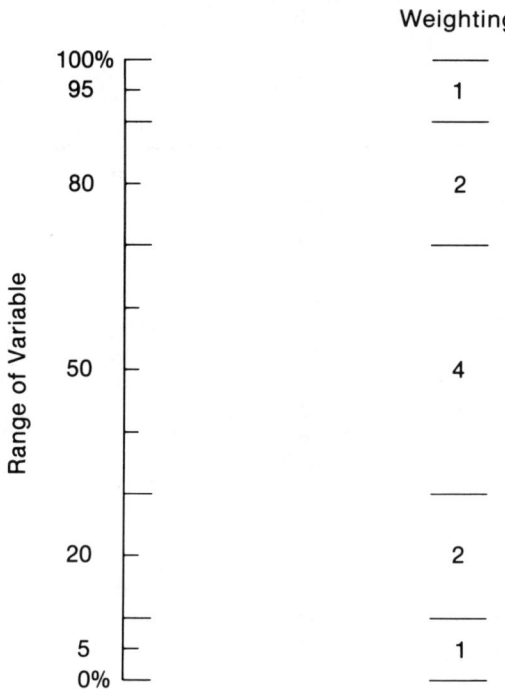

Figure 9-6. Relative weighting of random numbers used in Table 9-3

The column in Table 9-3 labeled "random number" gives ranges of random numbers that represent the expected likelihood that the corresponding scenario will be selected (Figure 9-6). These must be used in conjunction with a table of random numbers (Table 9-4). For example, if the random number 17 appears in conjunction with the sales scenario, the 80 percent estimate scenario of estimated sales is used. To illustrate how the data in Tables 9-3 and 9-4 are used to generate IRR cases for calculation, I provide two examples (Figure 9-7). About fifty cases are sufficient to yield a reasonably smooth ogive (Figure 9-8).

There are four points to remember about the second method to calculate an IRR probability distribution:

1. It is more work than the first method, requiring about half a day to calculate fifty IRR values using a programmable pocket calculator.
2. Although it is practical to calculate a few ogives with a

TABLE 9-4. Selection of Random Numbers Used to Generate Input Cases for Monte Carlo IRR

Case	1 Sales	2 Mfgr. Cost	3 Devel. Exp.	4 Oper. Cost	5 Capital
A	59	07	58	89	34
B	45	57	61	32	95
C	92	13	36	42	49
D	80	26	86	40	99
E	16	23	90	24	61
F	26	52	78	14	33
G	87	99	29	90	69
H	31	42	45	67	92
I	81	69	17	32	94
J	83	23	29	36	72
K	01	94	82	10	55
L	13	91	85	22	43
M	00	51	63	46	67
N	33	37	88	89	24
O	83	71	12	04	85
P	07	90	02	50	05
Q	15	28	77	82	86
R	62	90	42	04	75
S	16	84	77	88	89
T	34	56	53	62	37

pocket calculator, if this more flexible and general method is to be used frequently, it probably should be programmed on a business computer to reduce the tedium of manual calculation.

3. It permits use of alternative scenarios for the five estimated quantities that are both asymmetrical about the base case (for instance, the sales assumptions in Figure 9-5) and non-Gaussian.
4. If the likelihood of occurrence of alternate scenarios is different than 10%-20%-40%-20%-10% (used in Figure 9-6), other ranges of random numbers can be used. There can be more or fewer than five scenarios for any of the five estimated quantities.

There are more elaborate variations on the Monte Carlo method in which, for instance, each sales scenario carries a dif-

Case A

QUANTITY	YEAR (N) / DERIVATION	1	2	3	4	5	6	7	8	9	10
1 COMPANY SALES	ESTIMATE PLAN			2	2.4	2.88	3.46	4.15	4.98	4.98	4.15
2 MANUFACTURING COST	ESTIMATE 35% OF 1			0.7	0.84	1.01	1.21	1.45	1.74	1.74	1.45
3 DEVELOPMENT EXPENSE	ESTIMATE PLAN	0.5	0.5								
4 OPERATING EXPENSE	ESTIMATE 22% OF 1			0.44	0.53	0.63	0.76	0.91	1.09	1.09	0.91
5 CAPITAL EXPENDITURES	ESTIMATE PLAN	1.0									

Case K

QUANTITY	YEAR (N) / DERIVATION	1	2	3	4	5	6	7	8	9	10
1 COMPANY SALES	ESTIMATE 95% HIGH			3	4	5	7	10	15	20	20
2 MANUFACTURING COST	ESTIMATE 50% OF 1			1.5	2	2.5	3.5	5	7.5	10	10
3 DEVELOPMENT EXPENSE	ESTIMATE 80% HIGH	0.7	0.7								
4 OPERATING EXPENSE	ESTIMATE 17% OF 1			0.51	0.68	0.85	1.19	1.70	2.55	3.40	3.40
5 CAPITAL EXPENDITURES	ESTIMATE PLAN	1.0									

Figure 9-7. Two IRR input examples for Monte Carlo probability method

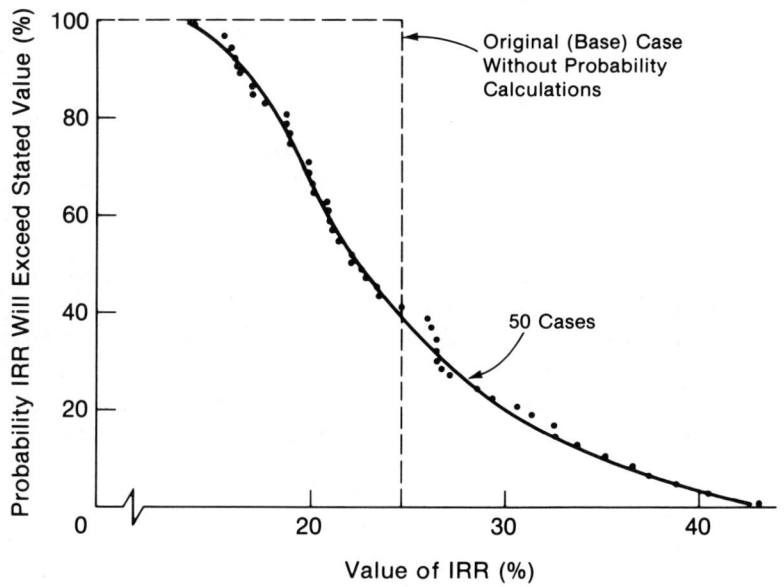

Figure 9-8. Monte Carlo Ogive

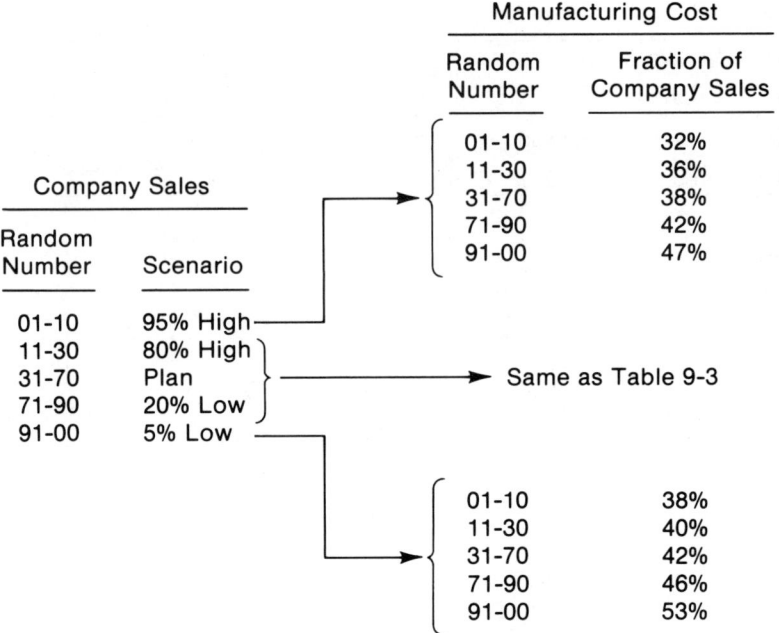

Figure 9-9. Illustration of more elaborate Monte Carlo method, in which the randomly selected sales scenario alters the choices for other input variables

ferent distribution of manufacturing, development, operating, and capital expense estimates. One example of such an elaborated model is illustrated in Figure 9-9: The highest sales scenario produces a selection of manufacturing cost scenarios with lower costs (to reflect the economies of scale), and the lowest sales scenario produces a selection of manufacturing cost scenarios with higher costs (to reflect manufacturing inefficiency caused by small volume). These elaborations are desirable if your company is carrying out many new product development programs or if you want greater realism in the financial model. This greater realism requires a more extensive computer program.

HIGHLIGHTS IRR ogives are useful for portraying the uncertainty of a new product development program.

Two easy ways to calculate IRR distributions are the Gaussian and the Monte Carlo methods.

The Gaussian method is quick but limited.

The Monte Carlo method is flexible.

Both methods produce answers that depend entirely upon your initial assumptions (the top five lines of the Profit MAP and the frequency distributions); so these assumptions must be both realistic and clearly stated.

As long as the uncertainty associated with each of the five estimated quantities can be described quantitatively, it is possible with either method to derive a distribution of expected values of IRR.

FURTHER READING

C. L. Gancer. "Is that New Product Worth Developing?" *Machine Design*, April 18, 1974, pp. 118–123.
    This is a brief article with an example of a different computer-based approach to considering the probability of financial return.

V. H. Herbert, Jr., and A. Bisio. "Venture Analysis: The Assessment of Uncertainty and Risk." Chap. 29, pp. 365–380, in R. R. Rothberg, ed., *Corporate Strategy and Product Innovation*, 2nd ed. New York: Free Press, 1981.
    This is a good discussion of the sensitivity of DCF, including some pointers on ways to present results to top management.

D. B. Hertz. "Risk Analysis in Capital Budgeting." *Harvard Business Review*, September–October 1979, pp. 169–181.
    This classic, excellent article describes the Monte Carlo method.

L. Winer. "A Profit-Oriented Decision System." Chap. 26, pp. 348–359, in R. R. Rothberg, ed., *Corporate Strategy and Product Innovation*. New York: Free Press, 1976.
    Winer discusses use of discounted cash flow and presents some other approaches to handling uncertainty.

Part 5

TEAMWORK

Unless you are going to do the entire job alone, you will have to work with others. How are you going to get your profitable new product idea into the world? In general, meaningful new products emerge only from corporate teams of dozens, if not hundreds, of people working together. New product (and other) efforts are much more successful when harmony is promoted in such teams. I examine in Chapter 10 the crucial role that top management can play. Then I look in Chapter 11 at some typical problems you can expect. In Chapter 12, I describe ways you can improve teamwork.

10

The Role of Top Management

KEY POINTS

Top management must participate in the initiation of new product development.

Corporate top management can use the annual planning cycle to foster teamwork on new product development efforts.

New product development phases can help clarify responsibilities.

Top management should establish an activity flow procedure.

Top management must periodically review new product development efforts.

ANNUAL PLANNING CONTEXT

Top management must lay the basis for teamwork within the corporation. They are clearly responsible for establishing the strategic framework, which I discussed in Part 1. In general, top management understands the requirement for setting a strategic context and accepts responsibility for it. However, once new product development efforts are underway, some top managements become involved again only when difficulties arise. This is a deplorable situation because the opportunity for top management to have a significant influence on a new prod-

Top management must participate in new product development initiation.

uct development program is much greater in the early phases of the program than in the later phases. I will explain how to assure appropriate top management participation throughout the life of a new product development program. First, I will describe a typical corporate annual planning cycle and indicate the involvement of top management in that activity.

Many corporations have formalized annual planning cycles. A typical cycle is illustrated in Figure 10-1. Corporate management provides annual guidance approximately six months prior to the beginning of the year for which a plan is being developed. This guidance is general, usually indicating broad macroeconomic trends as well as political, labor, and social issues that may affect the corporation. In the light of this, the corporate guidance will suggest a profit target and perhaps a sales growth target that the corporation should strive for in the following year.

Corporate annual planning helps build teamwork.

Shortly after the corporate guidance is provided, each business unit, for instance, a division, provides its order forecasts for the year being planned. Corporate management reviews these and suggests upward or downward revisions, as appropriate, in the context of the previously provided corporate guidance. After that, each of the business units assembles heavily detailed plans for the following year. Within these plans, some of the business units will also identify the specific new product development programs in which they will engage. Finally, the phase 2 plans may be adjusted somewhat, and prior to the start of the planning year, a phase 3 plan is committed to writing. It is the phase 3 plan against which business unit management is measured during the plan year.

During the plan year, reforecasts are made to reflect the reality of what is happening. However, in the year following the year that was planned, a phase 4 planning activity often occurs. This is a comparison of what actually occurred in the plan year against the previously approved phase 3 plan.

An annual planning cycle such as this assures that product development efforts are broadly coupled to top management thinking. These planning cycles assure that the required cooperation between departments and business units is identified systematically. Continuing reviews of new product programs, which are discussed later, assure that top management remains coupled to the process.

Also as a part of the annual planning cycle, corporate management must examine the plans of business units that do not have direct responsibility for external sales, for instance, the corporate research group. This kind of review, providing it is

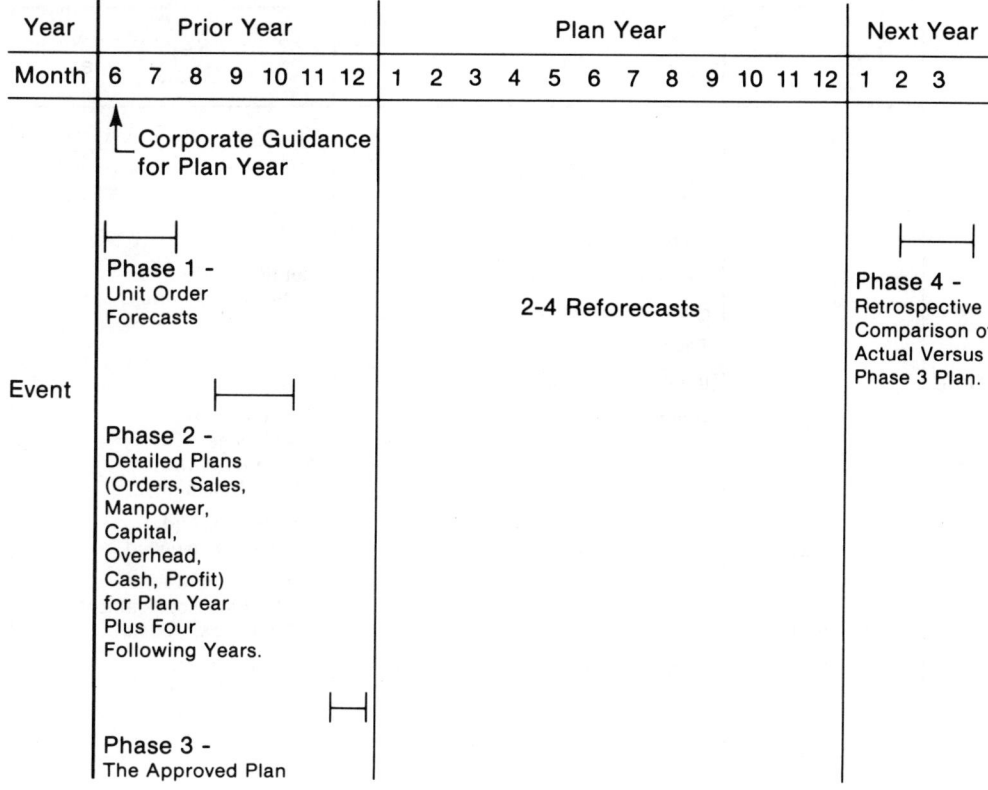

Figure 10-1. Typical annual planning cycle

done properly, also lays the basis for teamwork and integrative activities. One of the ways this integration can be accomplished is to have representatives of all the business units participate in the review of the corporate research plan. This procedure helps assure that at least some of the business units perceive planned activities in the corporate research department as useful.

ESTABLISHING NEW PRODUCT DEVELOPMENT PHASES

Each company has to have its own logical process for developing new products. In this section I review several ways to look

Key Functional Group	Activities	Key Goals
Research	Idea	
	Exploratory Research & Feasibility Demonstration	
	Product Development	
Engineering	Market Research & Business Plan	Identify Profit-Making Scenario
	Product Design & Pilot Plant	
	Tooling & Production Engineering	
	Initial Production	
	Commercialization	Create Market Awareness, Test Product in Use, Few Models
	Full-Scale Production & Market Expansion	Gain Share, Add Models as Needed
Marketing with Manufacturing	Product Maturity	Maintain Share, Introduce Replacement, Some New Models
	Product Obsolescense & Decline	Profit, Drop Marginal Models

Time ↓

Figure 10-2. Technical innovation route to market success

Establishing phases can clarify responsibilities.

at the process. Comparing your company's process with these will improve your understanding and may point out ways you can improve your process. Figure 10-2 illustrates the activities typically required to bring a technical innovation to the market and have it result in corporate profits. Assuming that the corporation is organized in a functional manner, which will be discussed in more depth in the next chapter, we can see how the lead responsibility has to move from one functional department to another as the new product development effort moves from one activity phase to another.

Figure 10-3 lists five ways various authors have enumerated phases of the new product development process. The first column is similar to the breakdown in Figure 10-2. The second column omits all product development activities prior to commercialization. The last three provide five, six, and seven phases to break up the continuum that runs from idea incep-

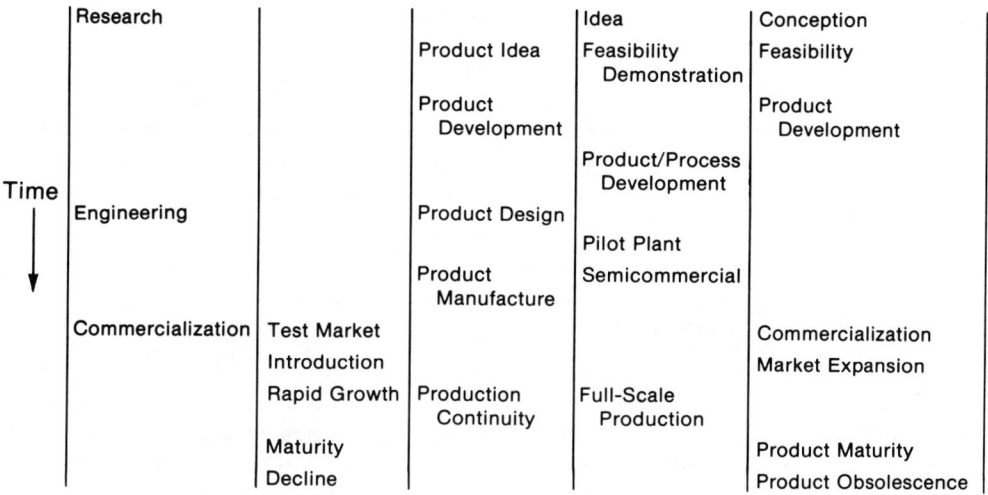

Figure 10-3. Phases of new product development

tion to eventual product decline. Table 10-1 provides more complete detail for the righthand column in Figure 10-3. It is to your advantage to establish a system of phases such as these because it clarifies departmental responsibilities. It also assures that systematic reviews are conducted at various checkpoints to provide scrutiny of the new product development effort. Table 10-2 suggests the kind of relationships that should exist between profit planning, as discussed in Part 4, and the materials being discussed in this and the next two chapters.

In many situations, there are not really sharp lines between these phases. This blurring will be more common in the smaller company than in the larger company. In the larger company, moving from one phase to another can frequently mean transferring responsibility for the new product development effort from one business unit to another. If this transfer is done prematurely, without a well-developed technical understanding and a demonstration of feasibility, the receiving department will not be particularly receptive and may very well kill the effort. If, however, the transfer of responsibility is accompanied by the transfer of several key people, including most usefully the principal advocate or product champion, this will help. If the growth potential of the new product development effort is fairly obvious, it is easier to build enthusiasm for taking on the development responsibility.

Transferring people helps build teamwork.

TABLE 10-1. Detailed Definitions and Objectives for One-Phase Structure

Phase	Definition	Objective
Conception	Project in which exploratory studies are made relative to new concepts.	Exploratory research to establish a completely new product line.
Feasibility	Project in which an exploratory study or some aspect of an exploratory study is expanded.	Define product parameters and examine market opportunities, determine manufacturing implications.
Product Development	Project directed toward the development of a product and/or application to satisfy a potential commercial opportunity.	Product is tailored to the application, taken through initial pilot scale-up and customer performance evaluation.
Commercialization	Project directed toward the field evaluation scale-up and market introduction.	Acceptance by customers establishes market potential and business decision to manufacture and include in standard product line.
Market Expansion	That stage in a product life cycle characterized by market expansion and rapid growth.	Maximize rate of sales and distribution. Maintain balance in capacity and market demand.
Product Maturity	That stage in a product life cycle characterized by product maturity & slow growth.	Maintain business & maximize profit over as long a time span as possible.
Product Obsolescence	That stage in a product's life cycle when product profit and sales growth are topping off & product or market is becoming obsolete.	Remove product from product line.

Sometimes the transfer of lead responsibility is also a transfer from one geographical location to another. For instance, a transfer may be from a corporate staff development activity to a divisional manufacturing site in some other location. In such a case it is particularly important to transfer people, which is usually done by moving people from the development location to the manufacturing site after the transfer has occurred. It is also feasible to move people from the manufacturing site to the

TABLE 10-2. Phase Dependency

	Early	Middle	Late
Uncertainty	Great	Some	Low
Financial Risk	Low	Large (for Tooling)	Should Be None or Low
Business Analysis	Simple (Back of Envelope)	Thorough (Done Before Tooling Costs Incurred)	Profit & Loss Statement
Organization	Existing	Venture Team or Functional	Functional

development site for three or six months or perhaps even a year prior to the scheduled transfer so that they become familiar with the program. The central point is that you should plan carefully before moving responsibility from one group to another, or one site to another, or in stepping from one phase of activity to another.

ESTABLISHING AN ACTIVITY FLOW

A major responsibility of top management, or of operating management if top management abdicates, is to establish an *activity flow procedure*. This procedure might be as illustrated in Figure 10-4. Each company has to establish a flow that is appropriate to it, but the characteristics and purposes of these flows are universal:

A standard activity flow helps.

1. To assure top management review
2. To assure that product development specifications are committed to writing, including the "must" and "want" characteristics; to reduce the likelihood that R & D is working in a vacuum by assuring that the technical and marketing data relative to the product are flowing into the R & D group
3. To provide schedule and budget control for the product development effort
4. To assure that joint reviews involving the marketing and R & D engineering groups are held.

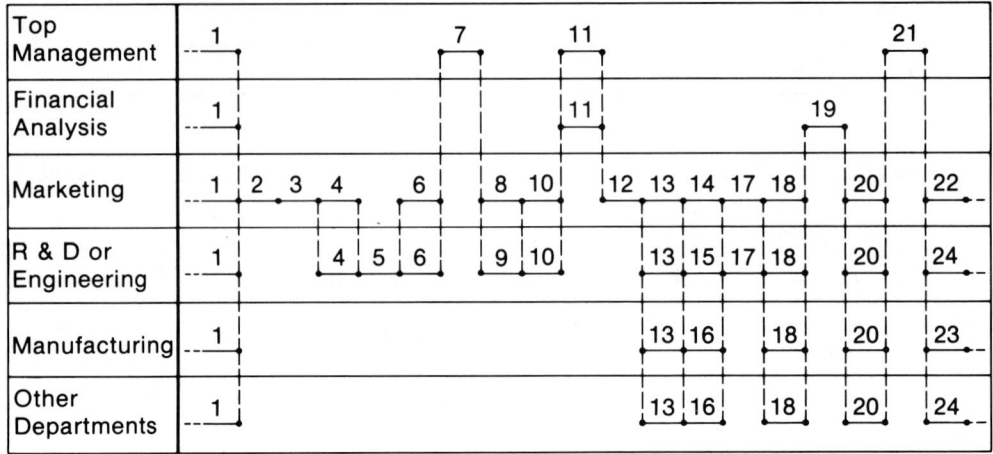

1 Someone identifies a potential opportunity
2 Need clarified
3 Preliminary idea write-up, with tentative "musts" & "wants"
4 Joint review of write-up
5 Preliminary feasibility study
6 Joint review of feasibility study
7 Authorize initial prototype
8 Preliminary market research
9 Build development prototype
10 Joint review & preliminary cost estimate
11 Review: Kill or authorize
12 Propose "must"/"want" attributes
13 Set production design specifications
14 Plan for detailed market research
15 Design & build production prototype
16 Preproduction planning
17 Conduct detailed market research
18 Joint review and detailed product planning
19 Do internal rate of return analysis
20 Formal recommendation to top management
21 Review: Kill or authorize
22 Create advertising, salesperson training, etc.
23 Production start-up
24 Assist marketing & manufacturing as required

Figure 10-4. An activity flowchart

The activity flow for your company will differ from the one in Figure 10-4. The phases in Figure 10-3, or the flowcharts cited at the end of this chapter (Clifton and Ffyfe, and McGuire) may suggest how to structure the most useful activity flow for your organization.

REVIEWS

It is absolutely essential that top management conduct periodic reviews of any significant new product development effort. These top management reviews are different than design reviews, held by the engineering department, for instance, which are also required. The hardest new product development decision to make is the decision to kill a project. A product champion, in common with others who are close to the new product effort, is necessarily an advocate of the effort. He or she must be enthusiastic about the effort and is therefore normally absolutely unable to kill it. The top management of the firm is also often unable to kill an effort that should be killed because they, by having authorized its initiation, are themselves sponsors of it. However, despite these biases, reviews are the best means to maintain objectivity.

Top management should conduct early reviews of a new product development effort to assure their enthusiasm and encouragement. Top management should do everything they can to assure that the effort is initiated and moving forward effectively. Later reviews, when the financial stakes are getting higher, especially prior to major tooling expense, must be conducted skeptically. In the large corporation people can be brought in from business units that are not directly involved, and they can conduct objective reviews. In the smaller corporation it is usually necessary to retain independent consultants to conduct this kind of skeptical, objective review. These reviews should examine the technical characteristics of the product and the progress toward meeting the established specifications within the development schedule and budget. These reviews must also look at whether external market changes are occurring. A constant question to consider is whether better investment opportunities are now available to the firm. Because the crucial factor in later reviews is objectivity, you may want independent, qualified consultants regardless of other resources available within your company. Five groups that certify consultants' competency are listed in the Appendix.

Early reviews can develop enthusiasm.

Later, objective reviews are essential.

The existence of a formalized activity flow will highlight that certain reviews are called for at certain points in the development process. One of the advantages of having established such an activity flow is that there can also be written standards for the criteria upon which the projects will be continued or discontinued. If these exist, it is easier to judge each new product development effort objectively at the critical reviews. To be useful and widely accepted, these criteria must result from the corporate strategy and profitability criteria, which have been set out earlier and which must have top management's concurrence. For instance, a new product development project might be required to have a 50 percent likelihood of an IRR greater than 20 percent.

For a decentralized corporation, for instance, one with divisions in separate locations, reviews may have to be held at different locations. These locations may vary from time to time depending on where the main work is being conducted. It is especially important that joint reviews involve participants from both locations if a project is moving from a corporate R & D lab to an operating division or from a development group to a manufacturing site.

HIGHLIGHTS The corporate annual planning cycle provides a vehicle for top management to involve all key personnel in the new product development effort, thus fostering teamwork.

A relatively standard definition of new product development phases can help identify required department interfaces, as can an activity flow chart.

Top management should use early reviews to develop enthusiasm.

Objective reviews are essential later in the new product development process.

FURTHER READING

W. J. Abernathy and J. M. Utterback. "Patterns of Industrial Innovation." *Technology Review*, June–July 1978, pp. 40–47.
This article discusses the corporate imperative to change innovation focus as a company grows and matures.

D. S. Clifton, Jr., and D. E. Fyffe. *Project Feasibility Analysis*. New York: Wiley, 1977.
Pages 3, 36, 86, and 125 contain four activity flowcharts.

H. Cohen, S. Keller, and D. Streeter. "The Transfer of Technology from Research to Development." *Research Management*, May 1979, pp. 11–17.
This study of eighteen IBM projects reveals that technical understanding, feasibility, advanced development overlap, existence of an advocate, and advanced technology activities in a development laboratory facilitate transfer.

L. A. Cox. "Industrial Innovation: The Role of People and Cost Factors." *Research Management*, March 1976, pp. 29–32.
> This is a brief review of costs in different phases of development.

P. F. Drucker. "The Innovative Company." *The Wall Street Journal*, February 26, 1982, p. 27.
> Drucker discusses how top management reviews should initially encourage innovative efforts and later should kill efforts that are no longer promising.

L. D. McGlauchlin. "Long-Range Technical Planning." *Harvard Business Review*, July–August 1968, pp. 54–64.
> How Honeywell coordinates its fundamental research with its engineering and marketing needs is the subject of this article.

E. P. McGuire. *Evaluating New-Product Proposals.* Conference Board report 604. New York: Conference Board, 1973.
> Two activity flowcharts appear on pages 2 and 3.

S. Myers and E. E. Sweezy. "Why Innovations Fail." *Technology Review*, March–April 1978, pp. 41–46.
> The authors discuss how management actions can block development.

E. B. Roberts. "Generating Effective Corporate Innovation." *Technology Review*, October–November 1977, pp. 25–33.
> Roberts stresses the need for a supportive environment for ideas to flourish.

E. B. Roberts and A. A. Frohman. "Strategies for Improving Research Utilization." *Technology Review*, March–April 1978, pp. 33–40.
> The authors provide a good conceptual framework for the relationships between the marketing and technology departments, sequenced by time phase.

M. D. Rosenau, Jr. *Successful Project Management.* Belmont, Calif.: Lifetime Learning Publications, 1981. Also "Project Management," a series of six videocassettes. Atlanta: Association for Media-Based Continuing Education for Engineers, 1981.
> This is a thorough, basic introduction to the techniques of project management, with extensive references to further reading.

W. White. "Effective Transfer of Technology from Research to Development." *Research Management*, May 1977, pp. 30–34.
> White briefly reviews some of the issues involved in transfer.

11

Organizational Issues

KEY POINTS Successful new product development efforts require at least four skills.

There are essentially three approaches to new product development organization within a corporation.

External ventures are another means to pursue new product development.

INGREDIENTS OF AN ORGANIZATION

A successful organization has to allow for many skills to be actively at work on the new product development effort. First, there has to be sponsorship by top management. This support provides general direction and a strategic context in which the new product development will be framed and assures that human and physical resources will be adequately supported by appropriate funding.

Second, there has to be a champion. Although you can develop a new product without this spark plug, it is a lot easier when the driving force is within the new product development group. It is much harder when top management imposes the drive for a new product on a reluctant group. The product champion is the kind of person who will work nights and weekends to overcome the many obstacles that inevitably threaten the new product development effort. Tom West, described in Tracy Kidder's book, *The Soul Of A New Machine*, is an example. The characteristics such a person typically exhibits include the following:

A champion keeps the new product development effort moving.

1. Technical competence
2. Company knowledge
3. Market knowledge
4. Drive and aggressiveness
5. Political astuteness

These personal characteristics are desirable, perhaps necessary, to move the new product development effort forward. However, there is often a serious problem of what to do with such a dedicated champion when the project ends, especially if unsuccessfully. Many times the champion is so dedicated to a project that is terminated that he or she leaves the corporation to carry on the project elsewhere.

Third, there has to be a generator of creative ideas. We tend to think that this person is a scientist or engineer. In fact, it may be a marketing person who recognizes a novel marketing twist, rather than a technological novelty, thus providing product differentiation.

The organization should allow for creative mavericks.

Fourth, there has to be a well-organized, disciplined manager who is capable of keeping a new product development effort project running smoothly. It is all too easy in a fit of enthusiasm to let the project specifications expand to encompass more than is required. A key role of the project manager is to be sure that the "must" and "want" specifications for the product are clearly understood. These attributes must be kept in mind by all the people at work on the effort, as must the schedule and development budget.

Someone has to keep the effort focused.

Several of these roles may be taken by a single person. Occasionally, one person takes them all, but that is unusual. Therefore, the purpose of the organization is to assure that the people with the required skills are organized to allow cooperative and effective work on the new product development effort.

ORGANIZATIONAL FORMS

A variety of new product organizational forms exists, including new product divisions, new product departments, new product managers, new product committees, venture teams, task forces, brand managers, and various ad hoc forms. Basically, however, within a corporation there are only three approaches to new product development organization: functional; project, which is really a venture team approach; and matrix, which includes the product line or brand manager approaches. A corporation can also engage in new product development by arranging an external joint venture with another company.

Regardless of organizational form, there is the issue of where the new product responsibility is put, as indicated in Figure 11-1. In a decentralized corporation, for instance, one that has independent divisions or business units, the responsibility for new product development can be assigned to each of those divisions (B in Figure 11-1). Alternatively, it can be the responsibility of a single corporate unit (A in Figure 11-1) or it can be both (C in Figure 11-1). The advantage of giving the responsibility to the divisions, or separate business units, is that they are tightly coupled with market reality. Thus, they are not likely to engage in any new product development effort that will not have commercial viability.

No organization form is perfect.

Conversely, they are not likely to take any long-range chances. The advantage of having corporate units responsible for new product development is that their charter is likely to be directly vested from top management and have better corporate support. But they often tend to work in an ivory tower or unrealistic marketing environment. Even if the development effort is successful, the corporate unit may have great difficulty transferring a development effort to an operating business unit.

Within a division, for instance, one that is functionally organized, the lead responsibility for new product development can lie with the marketing department (D in Figure 11-1), with the R & D or engineering department (E in Figure 11-1), or with a new product group (F in Figure 11-1). Each of these arrangements has strengths and weaknesses. The marketing people will be coupled with the outside world very well but will tend to take a short-range point of view. The marketing department may fail to appreciate opportunities that arise from new technological possibilities. The technical groups, R & D or engineering, are certainly going to exploit new technological possibilities, but they may do so unrealistically, inventing solutions looking for problems. A new product group may have the

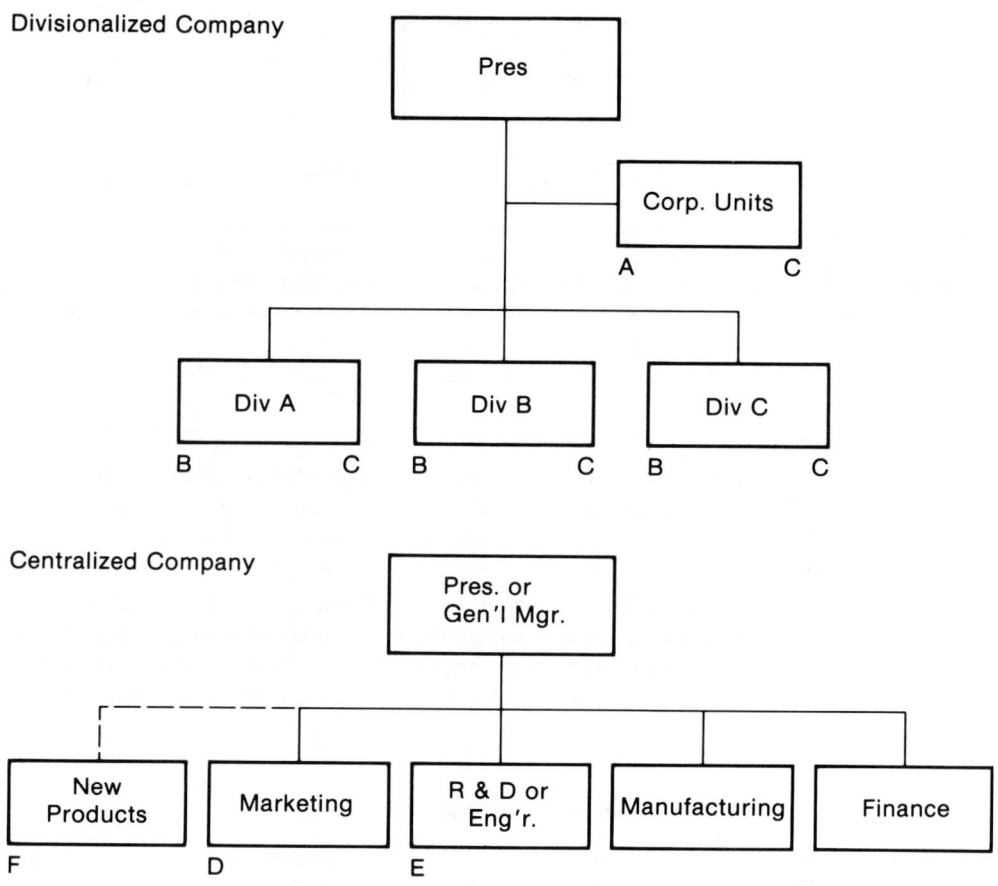

Figure 11-1. Location options for new product responsibility

blessing and support of the division president or general manager, but it may be unable to transfer its developments into the rest of the division due to "not invented here" (NIH) factors.

Functional Organization

A typical *functional organization* is shown in Figure 11-2. As indicated in the lower portion of Figure 11-1, there might also be a new product function within such a structure. This is a traditional organizational form and very good for managing a single product or product line. It groups enough people performing each function to assure that there is a critical mass. It

A functional organization is best for a narrow product line.

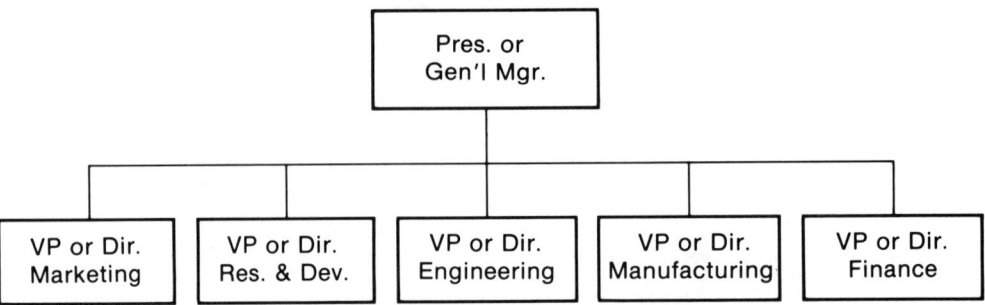

Figure 11-2. Functional organization

provides a professional career path within each of the functional disciplines. The difficulty this organizational form has in coping with new product development is the lack of institutional means to communicate from one department to another. That is, it is hard to get interdepartmental cooperation because formal mechanisms to assure it are available only through the president or general manager. In fact, there is more often hostility than cooperation between these separate departments.

Matrix Organization

A typical *matrix organization* is shown in Figure 11-3. This may also be called a *product manager* or *brand management organization*. It can be thought of as a functional organization with one additional functional unit, namely, product management.

In this kind of organization the product manager is responsible for cutting across the separate other functional boundaries to accomplish the goals he or she has in managing the product. Thus, when a new product is required within the product line, the product manager is responsible for coordinating the work or other functional specialties. The product manager is a project leader but lacks hierarchically assigned project personnel. Thus, the product manager decides what each of the other functional specialties will do, when it will be done, and the budget that will be allocated for it. Within the functional specialty, a decision is made as to who will be responsible to the product manager for that work package. Then that individual decides how he or she will satisfy the product manager's wishes. In actual practice the product manager, the functional

A matrix organization is best for a diverse product range.

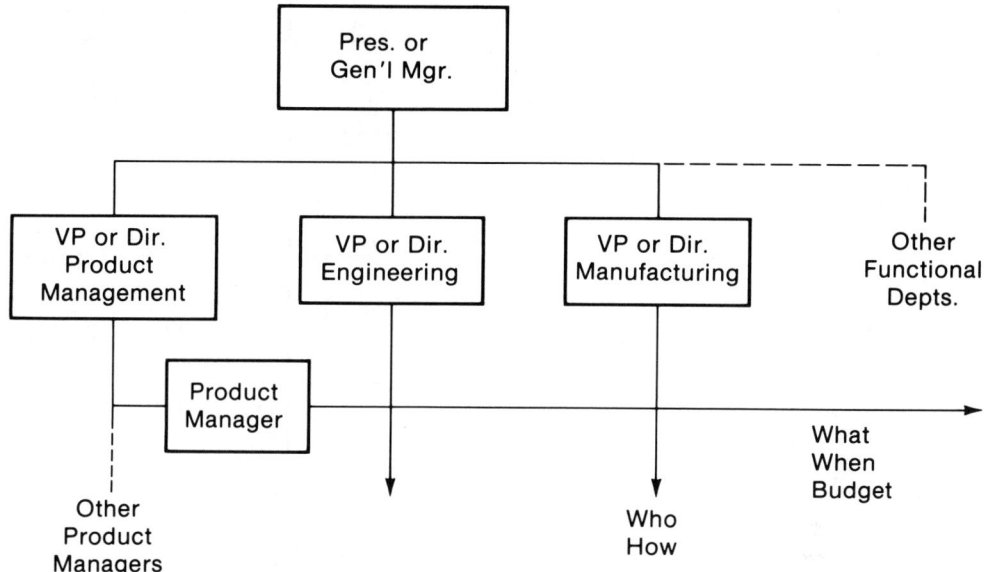

Figure 11-3. Matrix organization

manager, and the person designated to manage the work package negotiate the decisions as to what will be done, when it will be done, the budget, and how it will be accomplished.

This kind of matrix organization is particularly appropriate and useful where there are multiple product lines rather than a single product or product grouping. In the latter case the functional organization is more appropriate. One way to think about this distinction is to see in the functional organization the president or general manager as the product line manager. This can grow out of a company that has a matrix organization where one product line begins to become larger and larger. Very often the product manager and the people in the other functional specialties who have been contributing to it will spin off to become a separate business unit or division.

Venture Team

The *venture team*, often called an *internal venture*, may be thought of as a project management form of organization. The venture team typically consists of a marketing person, a technical person, and a manufacturing person. One of these may be

Internal venture teams are useful in large organizations.

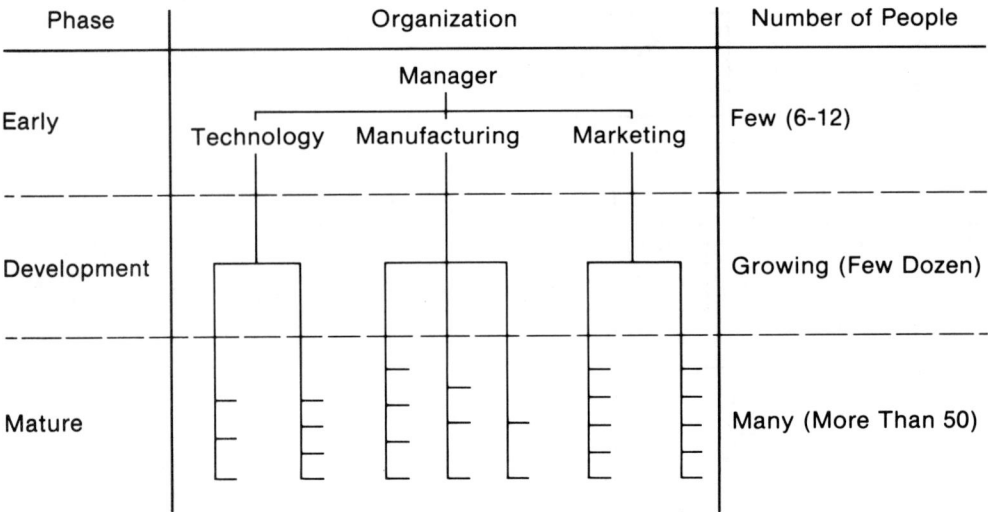

- **Figure 11-4.** Development of a venture organization

the manager of the venture or there might be a separate manager. There might also be a financial person as a member of the venture. As the venture progresses and matures, assuming it is successful, additional people would join, as illustrated in Figure 11-4. The typical venture is itself organized functionally. It may be housed within an organization with any of the previously discussed organizational forms. However, a venture team is more typically found within a large functional organization.

An internal venture or project group is broken apart from the rest of the functional organization because the large functional organization has too many vested interests and barriers to the development of a new idea. An observation by Machiavelli in *The Prince* highlights this: "It must be remembered that there is nothing more difficult to plan, more uncertain of success, nor more dangerous to manage than the creation of a new order of things. For the initiator has the enmity of all who would profit by the preservation of the old institutions, and merely lukewarm defenders in those who would gain by the new ones." A new idea will destroy whatever harmony exists and often be perceived by the vested interests as threatening because it forces change. In addition, product champions are often individualistic persons or mavericks, so they do not fit well within organizational constraints. Nevertheless, many of

TABLE 11-1. Some Innovations That Occurred Outside the Existing Industry

New Product	Innovator	Altered Organization/Industry
Nylon	DuPont	Silk
Instant Photos	Polaroid	Kodak, Ansco
Transistors	Texas Instruments	General Electric, RCA
Xerography	Haloid	IBM, Addressograph Multigraph
Light Bulb	Edison	Sperm Oil
Airplane	Wright Brothers	Transportation

the best, very clever new product ideas have come from innovative people who were not part of existing businesses in that field. Table 11-1 illustrates that some significant innovations have come from outside the leading company in various businesses. By encouraging internal ventures, large companies are now trying to assure that they can nurture innovative ideas and make them commercial successes.

Innovations often originate outside the leading company in a field.

Thus, many innovative companies in the United States (for instance, 3M and DuPont) have encouraged internal ventures. They are trying to obtain the combination of speed, dedication, and entrepreneurial spirit (which is usually found in a small, innovative company) and financial resources, labor resources, and facility support (which is more typically found in a large company). This organizational form is most appropriate where a new business area is being addressed and a new technology is required. In general, efforts with these characteristics are not handled well by an existing organization and are threatening to it. An alert top management may establish one or a few internal ventures to allow the small company spirit and attitude to develop. The venture team is thus insulated from the rest of the ongoing business but has the required support.

Internal ventures have been extensively reported upon, and there are many citations for further reading at the end of this chapter. However, there are a few points that should be highlighted:

1. Internal ventures should have the support and encouragement of top management, which establishes the criteria and strategic framework into which they fit.
2. Each venture should be judged against generalized crite-

ria, for IRR and growth opportunity, in a reasonably consistent and uniform way.

3. The entire process should be encouraged, with multiple sources of potential internal sponsorship available to a champion or initiator of a venture.
4. The venture leader, at least in the earliest days of the venture, should be the champion of the idea or the driving force behind it, rather than somebody who was drafted to manage the effort but is not enthusiastic about it.
5. There should be several ventures underway at any given time because it will be necessary to abandon or kill some of them.
6. Ventures should be periodically reviewed.
7. When unpromising ventures are terminated, the people who initiated them should not be penalized or other people will not propose other ventures.

EXTERNAL VENTURES

There are several *external venturing* possibilities, such as making a capital investment in another firm or spinning off your own technology to others (for instance, by issuing licenses). The *joint venture* is one in which two companies, typically a large and a small one, form a third company. The large company provides financial resources, labor, and facilities and has access to capital and perhaps a significant distribution, sales, and service network available. The small company can bring in dedication and speed and perhaps has the new technology that is to be exploited and an entrepreneurial spirit. The company established to capitalize on these things is often fifty-fifty owned, but the larger company usually controls it.

HIGHLIGHTS Top management sponsorship, a product champion, a generator of creative ideas, and a good manager are all needed for successful new product development.

Within a corporation there are basically three approaches to organizing new product development and each has strengths and weaknesses.

Functional organization is best for a narrow product line.

Companies with a diverse range of products might do best with a matrix organization.

Large organizations often profit from using internal venture teams.

External ventures, including the joint venture and licensing, are another approach to new product development.

FURTHER READING

G. Benson and J. Chasin. *The Structure of New Product Organization.* New York: Amacom, 1976.
> This is a somewhat academic pamphlet, including a survey of how sampled firms were organized for new product development, but it does contain a thorough listing of the various options.

A. K. Chakrabarti. "The Role of a Champion in Product Innovation." *California Management Review,* vol. 17, no. 2 (Winter 1974), pp. 58–63.
> The role of a product champion was studied, with the finding that successful innovations occurred in sixteen of seventeen cases where a champion was present.

A. B. Cohen. "New Venture Development at DuPont." *Long Range Planning,* June 1970, pp. 7–10.
> This brief article describes the venture that spawned Riston.

M. Hanan. "Corporate Growth Through Venture Management." *Harvard Business Review,* January–February 1969, pp. 43–61.
> This is a thorough article on the venture team approach to new product development, with a good flow chart.

R. M. Hill and J. D. Hlavacek. "The Venture Team: A New Concept in Marketing Organization." *Journal of Marketing,* vol. 36 (July 1972), pp. 44–50.
> Based on a field study of one hundred venture teams, the authors suggest that a venture team may be better than a conventional marketing department for managing innovative new products.

R. M. Hill and J. D. Hlavacek. "Learning from Failure." *Califor-*

nia *Management Review*, vol. 19, no. 4 (Summer 1977), pp. 5–16.
> The authors offer ten specific recommendations for venture management.

J. D. Hlavacek. "Toward More Successful Venture Management." *Journal of Marketing*, vol. 38 (October 1974), pp. 56–60.
> Hlavacek makes seven suggestions for more successful venture management.

J. D. Hlavacek and V. A. Thompson. "The Joint Approach to Technology Utilization." *IEEE Transactions on Engineering Management*, vol. EM-23, no. 1 (February 1976), pp. 35–41.
> This is a study of nineteen joint venture companies, usually formed by a smaller technology-based parent and a larger parent with marketing and financial resources.

D. S. Hopkins. *Options in New-Product Organization*. Conference Board report 613. New York: Conference Board, 1974.
> This is an excellent, thorough report on the pros and cons of the various options for organizing.

R. M. Janowiak. "New Venture Management." *IEEE Transactions on Engineering Management*, vol. EM-23, no. 1 (February 1976), pp. 47–50.
> This is a brief and somewhat superficial discussion of venture management.

S. C. Johnson and C. Jones. "How to Organize for New Products." Chap. 15, pp. 188–204, in R. R. Rothberg, ed., *Corporate Strategy and Product Innovation*, 2nd ed. New York: Free Press, 1981.
> This is a reprint of a 1957 *Harvard Business Review* article that focuses on appropriate departmental responsibilities.

T. Kidder. *The Soul of a New Machine*. Boston: Little, Brown, 1981.
> This is a popular and very readable account of the development of the Data General MV/8000 minicomputer.

R. W. Peterson. "New Venture Management in a Large Company." *Harvard Business Review*, May–June 1967, pp. 68–76.
> The DuPont approach to venture management is the subject of this article.

E. B. Roberts. "Technical Venture Strategies," videotape lecture. Cambridge, Mass.: Massachusetts Institute of Technology, 1975.
> This is an excellent overview of all forms of venture management, with much detail on the 3M approach.

B. Twiss. "Organization for Innovation." Chap. 7, pp. 176–205, in B. Twiss, *Managing Technological Innovation*, 2nd ed. London: Longman, 1980.

This is a complete review of the various options and their strengths and weaknesses.

E. A. von Hippel. "Successful and Failing Internal Corporate Ventures; An Empirical Analysis." *Industrial Marketing Management*, vol. 6 (June 1977), pp. 163–174.

By a study of eighteen corporate ventures, the author concludes that three factors discriminate success from failure.

D. L. Wilemon and G. R. Gemmill. "The Venture Manager as Corporate Innovator." *California Management Review*, vol. 16, no. 1 (Fall 1973), pp. 49–56.

This is a study of the problems encountered by venture managers.

12

Improving Interface Harmony

KEY POINTS Friction between individuals, especially between those in different departments, is common in new product development.

The problem is usually most damaging when disharmony exists between the R & D or engineering departments and the marketing department.

Teams and task forces can be used to help build harmony.

THE DISHARMONY PROBLEM

It is unrealistic to expect harmony.

I have pointed out the difficulty in identifying market needs, in devising clever solutions to satisfy those needs, and in finding a way to do this that assures profit. Another new product development problem is coping with the traditional conflict between the marketing and the R & D or engineering departments. No series of procedures or analyses can ever eliminate this problem. Figure 12-1 illustrates the three key interfaces that each of the principal operating departments or functions has with others. Each of these interfaces has conflict. Without minimizing any of these conflicts, it has been found that teamwork between the marketing department and the technical departments is crucial for new product development success.

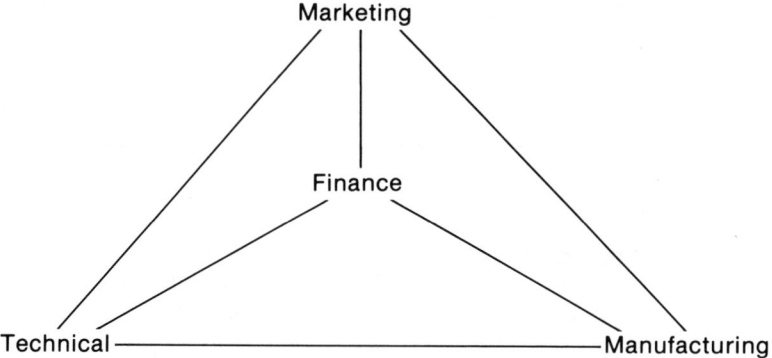

Figure 12-1. Departmental interfaces that often exhibit organizational conflict

Table 12-1 highlights these issues from the point of view of the research and development department, which is very similar to that of the engineering department. In their relations with the marketing (and often sales) department, there is at the very basis of everything a different time orientation. Market-oriented people, tied to the commercial world, want the new product now (if not yesterday) and are most interested in a low price. In addition, marketing personnel will often stress styling and appearance. The technical departments are oriented to the world of science and technology, want enough time to do their own thorough analysis and laboratory investigation, strive for technical perfection regardless of the commercial necessity, and do not particularly care what the appearance is as long as the functions are elegantly performed. In general, technical people do not speak the same language as marketing personnel.

Each department has a natural orientation.

Even within any one department there are sources of organizational conflict. For instance, in the research department there will be a managerial orientation, an applied research orientation, and a fundamental research orientation. People typical of one of these orientations will frequently be at loggerheads with people typical of another orientation.

The extensive study by Souder cited at the end of the chapter is one of many that crystallizes the central issues:

1. The marketing and R & D parties often disagree.
2. Nearly all firms exhibit this, but the problem is worse in large firms and those with centralized R & D structures.

TABLE 12-1. Some Sources of Organizational Conflict for the R & D Department

Other Departments	Their Emphasis	R&D Emphasis
Corporate Management	Business Profit	Technology Money for R&D
Marketing & Sales	Quick Response Low Price Appearance	Thorough Analysis Technical Perfection Function
Manufacturing	Few Variations Current Technology	Optimized Features Advanced Technology

3. The degree of harmony, joint involvement, and felt partnership between R & D or marketing is a significant determinant of project success.

4. Special mechanisms and management attention are needed to overcome these differences.

5. Those firms that are most successful at innovation have organizational climates that promote collaboration by emphasizing frequent face-to-face exchanges (rather than administrative hierarchies or paperwork systems).

You can thus see why I stressed in the previous chapter the role of top management and emphasized the use of reviews as a teamwork building mechanism.

PROMOTING HARMONY

Use teams and task forces to build harmony.

The first step is to recognize the disharmony problem. Do not pretend the problem is not real because you cannot see it. Some of the means by which harmony can be promoted are the use of teams, for instance, internal venture teams. Sometimes a marketing person and a technical person can be assigned to a task force to deal with some particular immediate problem, thus building team relationships. Working lunches and joint trips also provide opportunities for informal bonds to develop. Sending people from both departments to attend training seminars together is often a good way to improve teamwork. Per-

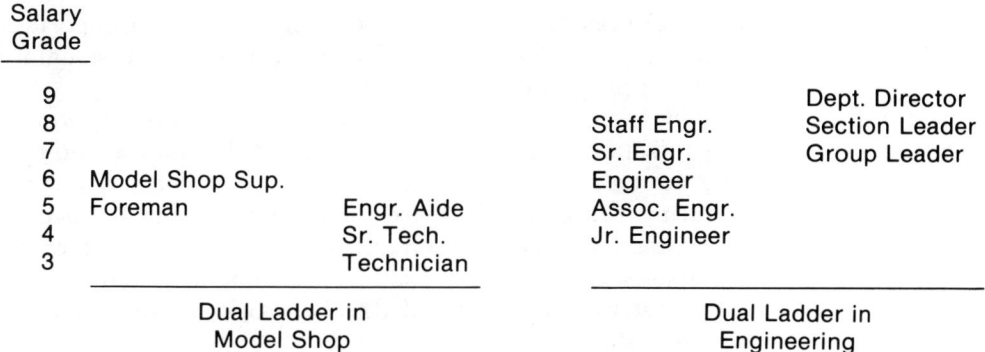

Figure 12-2. A dual ladder system

sonnel exchanges, where a marketing person is loaned to the engineering department, for instance, or a person from R & D is temporarily assigned to work in the marketing department, can help all parties develop a much better understanding.

Other joint activities, such as both marketing and the technical people participating in some aspect of market research, can often overcome difficulties. Recriminations frequently occur when marketing conducts market research and conveys negative findings back to the technical development people. If the technical inventor goes along on some marketing research visits to prospective customers, he or she will hear the evaluation directly. For this to work, you must be certain that the inventor will be willing actually to listen to what is being said and not become defensive or argumentative.

An equality of top management treatment also helps. A dual ladder, as illustrated in Figure 12-2, is important within a homogeneous group to provide both a technical and a managerial growth pattern. Equality between different departments is also important. It assures that a person carrying out a given level of responsibility within, say, the engineering department is treated like one with comparable responsibilities in the marketing department. Both people, carrying out equivalent responsibilities, should be in the same salary grade and be entitled to the same perquisites. They should have equivalent organizationally oriented incentives, for instance, salary, stock options, profit sharing, and office space. However, there must also be professionally oriented incentives peculiar to the specific department. For instance, scientists frequently wish to publish materials in scientific journals, attend scientific meetings, and

Top management must assure evenhanded treatment.

Venture teams can be very effective.

have laboratory equipment. These incentives are not important to somebody in marketing, but they too require professional incentives appropriate to their discipline.

There is an inherent value of the internal venture approach to organization. At least at the inception of the venture and certainly through its early life, the marketing, technical, and manufacturing representatives are in intimate, frequent, face-to-face contact. The use of top management reviews, in which all participants in any new product development activity are jointly reviewed (and rewarded), also works to develop common goals that build harmony.

What do you do if disharmony persists? It is still possible to break down these barriers to effective teamwork by using organizational development consultants or industrial psychologists. These experts can focus on the specific substantive problems, identify the underlying emotional issues, and develop therapies to reduce these problems. As with other consultants, qualified experts can be located through the five certifying organizations listed in the Appendix.

HIGHLIGHTS Disharmony normally exists and must be expected in the course of new product development.

If tolerated, disharmony can result in failure of new product development efforts.

Conflict must be confronted early because it tends to escalate rapidly.

Techniques to improve harmony include teams, joint activities, exchange of personnel between departments, and reviews by top management.

FURTHER READING

S. K. Bhalla. "Make R & D Cheaper, Faster, Better, with Teamwork." *Industrial Research and Development*, September 1981, pp. 159–161.

This is a very brief article on using a team of research chem-

ists and engineers to follow a project from the laboratory to full-scale production.

A. D. Biller and E. S. Shanley. "Understanding the Conflicts between R & D and Other Groups." *Research Management*, September 1975, pp. 16–21.
> The authors suggest ways to improve intergroup relations despite sociocultural differences.

H. D. Bissell. "Research and Marketing—Rivals or Partners?" *Research Management*, May 1971, pp. 65–73.
> Bissell presents the views each department has of the other.

A. E. Brown and T. S. Osdene. "Twelve Ways to Improve R & D-Corporate Relations." *Research Management*, May 1970, pp. 183–190.
> This article provides useful prescriptions for harmony as well as some analysis of how disharmony arises.

P. A. Carroad and C. A. Carroad. "Strategic Interfacing of R & D and Marketing." *Research Management*, January 1982, pp. 28–33.
> This is a good discussion of using dyads to promote harmony.

L. R. Jauch. "Tailoring Incentives for Researchers." *Research Management*, November 1976, pp. 23–27.
> The care and feeding of the researcher is the topic of this article.

J. P. Monteleone. "How R & D and Marketing Can Work Together." *Research Management*, March 1976, pp. 19–21.
> This very brief discussion suggests joint teamwork.

E. D. Phelps. "Improving the Product Development Process." *Industrial Marketing Management*, vol. 6 (February 1977), pp. 47–52.
> This brief discussion emphasizes the need for frequent interaction between marketing and engineering.

B. P. Shapiro. "Can Marketing and Manufacturing Coexist?" *Harvard Business Review*, September–October 1977, pp. 104–114.
> This is a very lucid discussion of the special problems between two departments.

W. E. Souder. "An Exploratory Study of the Coordinating Mechanisms Between R & D and Marketing as an Influence on the Innovation Process." National Technical Information Service, PB 279366, 1977; "Effectiveness of Product Development Methods." *Industrial Marketing Management*, vol. 7 (October 1978), pp. 299–307; "Promoting an Effective R & D/Marketing

Interface." *Research Management*, July 1980, pp. 10–15; "Disharmony Between R & D and Marketing." *Industrial Marketing Management*, vol. 10 (February 1981), pp. 67–73.

> The first citation is a basic study of 116 innovation projects in 18 firms, concluding that the two parties must achieve organizational integration. All four citations suggest ways to promote harmony.

W. E. Souder and A. K. Chakrabarti. "The R & D/Marketing Interface: Results from an Empirical Study of Innovation Projects." *IEEE Transactions on Engineering Management*, vol. EM-25, no. 4 (November 1978), pp. 88–93.

> This is an academic analysis of some of the data from the basic study in the previous reference.

M. F. Wolff. "When You Have to Get Up and Speak." *Research Management*, March 1982, pp. 11–12.

> Wolff discusses problems technical people have when they try to communicate with nontechnical people and suggests steps to take to improve this vital communication.

H. C. Young. "Effective Management of Research-Market Teams." *Research Management*, March 1979, pp. 7–12.

> Young tells how to use dyads and discusses problems in their use.

Part 6

SUMMARY

The last part of the book suggests where and how you should look for profitable new product opportunities yourself and identifies other steps for you to take.

13

Concluding Remarks

There are universal success criteria.	**KEY POINTS**
There is a way of thinking you can use to pursue potential opportunities.	
Keep my highlights in mind as you pursue new product development.	

NEW PRODUCT SUCCESS CRITERIA

The following list highlights the key criteria for new product success. These are all market driven, that is, market conditions provide the basic opportunity for a successful, profitable new product.

1. Replaces existing product
   - Better design
   - Lower price
2. Supplements existing product
   - Supplies demand not presently met by others
3. Serves a new market
   - Fills need not previously recognized
   - Fills need created by changed conditions

I do not want to denigrate technological innovation and cleverness. However, the blind intellectual search for new technology belongs in the research laboratory, not in the commercial world. "Market astuteness may be more critical than research competence or technical brilliance.... The failures occurred not mainly in research—most projects achieved their technical goals—but in marketing: customers didn't want to buy the product, at least not at the price they would have to pay. The likelihood that an innovation will succeed commercially seems to depend on cross-fertilization between a company's research and marketing staffs." (*Fortune*, January 25, 1982, p. 67). In the commercial world, technological cleverness must be aimed at producing products directed toward unfilled market needs. Fruitful technical work is done when there is a plan to make more money by developing the innovation rather than by investing in an alternative. Innovative efforts in profitable new product development serve the following functions:

- Scan new technology to lower the cost or improve the features of existing products.
- Develop clever solutions to fill market needs validated by market research.

Other success factors involve such things as a commitment by top management, a competent new product development champion, a cooperative functioning team, and clearly defined and stable new product development objectives that are well understood.

FUTURE OPPORTUNITIES

How do *you* come up with profitable new products? The key is to be constantly sensing and looking at the outside world. A constant questioning has to exist. What am I observing and how can I improve it? Many times the improvement will be possible but there is no way to make money at it, in which case you should not proceed further. Wherever change is occurring, opportunities are being created. For instance, as the cost of energy increases, opportunities are being created for new energy-saving products. As an example, a new refrigeration controller for trucks carrying fresh produce can save enough fuel in one year to pay for itself. Or as the cost of medical treatment is skyrocketing, alternatives become viable.

The search for these kinds of opportunities requires an open and questioning mind. Reading widely is a big help. In particular, the *New York Times* and the *Wall Street Journal* provide excellent coverage of general business news. In addition, business publications such as *Business Week*, *Fortune*, and *Forbes* provide other useful input. But it is not enough merely to read. You must read, visit others, observe, and constantly ask, Is there some problem somewhere and is there some way we can solve that problem?

HIGHLIGHTS

This last section consists of a listing of the most important points I have made. It provides a quick overview and may be used as a refresher.

- Know why your company should (or should not) engage in new product development.
- Understand the strategic model used by your company, and remember that this provides only a framework for action rather than a specific guide.
- Understand your own company's strengths and weaknesses.
- Understand the markets you serve and related opportunities.
- Constantly review your strategy, competitive position, development status, and market situation.
- Long-range profit growth will require new product development.
- Profitable new product development requires (1) a strategic framework, (2) a market idea or concept, (3) an innovative idea for a product to satisfy that market need, (4) a profit plan, and (5) teamwork.
- Success is never guaranteed; so good management concentrates limited resources on a small number of potentially important opportunities.
- Aim at filling real market needs.
- Plan to be number one or number two in the market or your niche.
- Evaluate the potential market carefully using brainstorming, quick estimates, on-line information retrieval, or market research.
- Market research must be used before major investments are made to answer four crucial questions: (1) Is the product concept functionally suitable? (2) Does the product offer

performance advantages? (3) Is there an economic incentive for buyers? (4) Is the available business attractive to us?

Market research techniques include multiattribute utility analysis, focus groups, data base searching, personal and telephone interviews, and mailed questionnaires.

Although market research can be performed by either company personnel or an outside firm, the latter are invariably more objective.

Establish a supportive environment for new ideas, which should be sought both inside and outside the company.

A new technological development, new legislation, and economic changes may provide an alert company the chance to develop a new product or successfully reactivate a previously abandoned development effort.

Licensing may allow a company to capitalize upon an idea developed elsewhere.

Evaluate new product ideas carefully and skeptically: Can it be made? Can it be sold at a profit?

Use checklists and consider the fifty-four evaluation issues.

Use objective skeptics to help evaluate ideas.

Have a plan to make money, using the Profit MAP (or similar format) to determine the internal rate of return for the proposed program.

Remember that the calculated internal rate of return is an estimate and depends on assumptions; so judgment must also be used.

Ogives of the internal rate of return are a useful way to portray the uncertainty of a new product development program, and these may be calculated by either of two methods: The Gaussian method, which is quick but limited, and the Monte Carlo method, which is flexible.

Involve top management through the annual planning cycle or reviews to assure support and encouragement and to help promote teamwork.

A relatively standard definition of new product development phases can help identify required department interfaces, as can an activity flowchart.

Organize appropriately and recognize that each approach has strengths and weaknesses.

Encourage teamwork and cooperation and quickly confront the disharmony or conflict that are normal before they escalate by using teams, joint activities, personnel exchanges, and top management reviews.

If at first you don't succeed, keep trying.

Appendix
Contacts for Additional Assistance

CONSULTANTS

Associations that certify management consulting *companies*:

1. Association of Consulting Management Engineers
   230 Park Avenue
   New York, NY 10017
   (212) 697-9693

2. Association of Management Consultants
   P.O. Box 1235
   Saratoga, CA 95070
   (408) 867-5293

Associations that certify *individual* management consultants:

1. Association of Professional Consultants
   Suite 106
   567 San Nicholas Drive
   Newport Beach, CA 92660
   (714) 760-9601

2. Institute of Management Consultants
   19 West 44th Street
   New York, NY 10036
   (212) 921-2885

3. Society of Professional Management Consultants
   16 West 56th Street
   New York, NY 10019
   (212) 586-2041

PROFESSIONAL ASSOCIATIONS

1. American Marketing Association
   250 South Wacker Drive
   Chicago, IL 60606
   (312) 648-0536

2. Engineering Management Society
   Institute of Electrical and Electronics Engineers
   345 East 47th Street
   New York, NY 10017
   (212) 644-7900

3. Industrial Research Institute
   100 Park Avenue
   New York, NY 10017
   (212) 683-7626

4. Product Development and Management Association
   c/o C. Merle Crawford
   Graduate School of Business Administration
   University of Michigan
   Ann Arbor, MI 48109
   (313) 763-1327

Index

Acquisition *21*
Activity flow *147–149*
After-tax income *109–111*
Air bags *4–5*
Analytic instruments *74–75*
Annual plan *142–143*
Arthur D. Little *13*

Barriers to competition *89*
Boston Consulting Group *9–13*
Brainstorming *34, 50, 77*
Brand manager *154, 156–157*

Camera lens *94–95*
Capital expenditures *106–111, 113*
Cases and examples
    air bags *4–5*
    analytic instruments *74–75*
    camera lens *94–95*
    CAT scanner *101*
    Concorde *6*
    currency inspection *34–36*
    electronic faucet *93–94*
    float glass *24–26, 29–30*
    Micralign *26–30*
    microdensitometer *59–60*
    photogrammetry *59–60*
    plastic lamina for glass lens *94–95*

pressure-sensitive adhesive *48*
Pringle's chips *49*
prototype device *57–58*
retroreflective sheeting *12*
shoplifting prevention *45–46*
ski manufacturing *5, 87*
Speak & Spell *76–77*
Starblast *46*
structural pressure-sensitive tape *48*
ultraviolet curing *52*
Z-tape *64–66*
Cash cow *11*
Cash flow *9, 101–121*
Cash trap *11*
Cash use. See Cash flow.
CAT scanner *101*
Champion, *145, 149, 152–153, 160, 174*
Checklists *81, 86–93*
Companies
    Arthur D. Little *13*
    Boston Consulting Group *9–13*
    DuPont *46, 74–75, 159*
    EMI *101*
    General Electric *8–9*
    Levi Strauss *46*
    Lockheed *51–52*
    McKinsey *5*

Index

Companies, (cont.)
  New York Times 89
  Perkin-Elmer 26-30
  Pilkington 24-26, 29-30
  Polaroid 39
  Proctor & Gamble 46, 49
  SDC 51
  Texas Instruments 76-77
  3M 159
  Wang Laboratories 46
Competition 8, 84-85, 89, 112
Concorde 6
Confidence 112
Conjoint analysis 60-62
Continuing costs 84
Consultants 22, 53, 57-60, 62-63, 68, 74, 77, 131, 149, 168
Criteria 21-22
Currency inspection 34-36

Data base. See Information retrieval.
DCF 23, 103-121
Depreciation 107-111
Development expense 84
Discount factors 111, 113
Discounted cash flow. See DCF.
Diversification 5-6
Dog 11
DuPont 46, 74-75, 159
Dyads 50, 52, 63, 166-167

EMI 101
Electronic faucet 93-94
Evaluation issues 91-93
Experience curve 9-12
External ventures 160

Fallacies 36-40, 47
Float glass 24-26
Focus group 62
Framework 18-24, 159
Functional organization 154-156

Gaussian method 126-129
General Electric 8-9

Harmony 52, 158, 164-168
Highlights 14, 29-30, 40, 53, 68-69, 78, 95-96, 120, 136-137, 150, 160-161, 168, 175-177

IDEA 76-77
Information retrieval 50-52, 66-67
Internal rate of return. See IRR.
Internal ventures 157, 166, 168
Interviews 63-67
Investment 32-33
IRR 24, 102-121, 124-137, 149, 160

Joint ventures 21, 154, 160

Legislation 3, 75
Levi Strauss 46
Licensing 21, 64, 77-78, 89
Life cycle 3, 13
Liquidated venture 111, 119-121
Lockheed 51-52
Lost profit of replaced product 84

Mail questionnaire 66, 68
Market research 34-36, 48-50, 53, 56-69, 106, 131, 167
Market segments 67
Market share 9, 12, 47, 50, 106
Matrix organization 156-157
McKinsey 5
Merger 21
Micralign 26-30
Microdensitometer 59-60
MMM. See 3M.
Monte Carlo method 126-137
Multiattribute utility analysis 60-62

Net present value. See NPV.
New York Times 89
NPV 24, 103, 111

Ogive 126-137
On-line information retrieval 50-52, 66-67
Organization 152-161

Patents 66, 83, 89-90
Payback 45-46, 103-104, 111

Perkin-Elmer *26–30*
Phases of new product
    development *143–148*
Photogrammetry *59–60*
Pilkington *24–26, 29–30*
Planning gap *7*
Plastic lamina for glass lens *94–95*
Polaroid *39*
Present value. *See* NPV.
Pressure-sensitive adhesive *48*
Pringle's chips *49*
Pricing *103, 119–120*
Probability *112, 125–137*
Problem idea *34, 37, 45–47, 50*
Proctor & Gamble *46, 49*
Product life cycle *3, 13*
Product manager *156–157*
Profit *7, 18–19, 101–121*
Profit MAP *102–121*
Profit margin *103*
Project management *149, 153, 158–160*
Prototype device *56–57*

Question mark *11*
Questionnaire *65–66*
Quick estimate *50–51*

Replaced product *84, 111–112*
Research. *See* Market research.
Retroreflective sheeting *12*
Return on investment. *See* ROI.
Reviews *142, 147–150, 160, 166, 168*
Risk *8, 50, 112–113, 126–127*
ROI *7, 24, 103–105, 114–115*

S-Curve *5*
SDC *51*
Segments *67*
Sensitivity *116*
Shoplifting prevention *45–46*
SIC codes *66–67*
Ski manufacturing *5, 87*
Solution idea *34, 37, 50, 73–78*
Speak & Spell *76–77*
Standard industrial classification.
    See SIC codes.
Star *11*
Starblast *46*
Stock price *38–40*
Strategic plan *18–21*
Strategy *1–14, 18–21, 149, 152, 159*
Structural pressure-sensitive
    tape *48*

Teamwork *52, 145, 164–168, 174*
Telephone interviews *66, 68*
Texas Instruments *76–77*
3M *159*
Triad *52*

Ultraviolet curing *52*
Uncertainty *84, 124–137*

Venture *21, 154, 157–160*

Wang Laboratories *46*
Working capital increase *108–111*

Z-tape *64–66*